Alive and Running

DEVOTIONS FOR ACTIVE PEOPLE

Alive and Running

DEVOTIONS FOR ACTIVE PEOPLE

Victoria Booth Demarest

WORD BOOKS, PUBLISHER
WACO, TEXAS

First Printing—October 1976
Second Printing—August 1977

Alive and Running: Devotions for Active People

ISBN 0-87680-482-2
Library of Congress catalog card number: 76-19528
Printed in the United States of America

*To all busy people who long for a
daily moment of spiritual relaxation
and meditation but are pressed by
the duties and demands of everyday life*

CONTENTS

FOREWORD

Victoria Booth Demarest is not only a well-qualified writer but also an experienced observer of the social, individual, and environmental conditions of the contemporary scene.

Her latest volume, *Alive and Running: Devotions for Active People*, should have a very wide and popular distribution for many reasons. It is composed of short discussions of everyday experiences which are sought after in religious writing today. It reflects the evangelical spirit of the author's famous grandfather, General William Booth, the founder of the Salvation Army, which transformed the spiritual atmosphere of the England of his day and continues to the present as a world-transforming force for spiritual renewal. It is written in simple language which communicates with both youth and age.

For people who have been so busy that God has become a lost thought in daily activity, a minute chapter night and morning from *Alive and Running* will not only reclaim his lost presence but also bring peace and contentment. For those who may be uncertain and confused, it provides a pattern for restoring their faith in an age, which having everything to live with, is falling apart because it has nothing to live for.

—Bishop Fred Pierce Corson
Past President,
Methodist World Council

INTRODUCTION

Since doing depends upon being, and since being the kind of persons we want to be and God wants us to be requires regular meditation and prayer, devotional literature that is "alive" and speaks to our present-day needs holds a place second to none in Christian writing.

STILLNESS

Be still, and know that I am God.—Psalm 46:10

Be silent, O all flesh, before the Lord.—Zechariah 2:13

In Cathedral Woods on the island of Monhegan, Maine, it is a meaningful experience to stand still and listen to the silence. Sunlight filters through the pillared spruce making patterns on the carpet of pine needles and on the drapery of giant ferns. Large gold and crimson toadstools make an altar of the banks of moss, and over all and through all is the overwhelming silence accented by the sudden chirp of a bird or a rustle of leaves. It is stillness that is awe-inspiring and like a call to worship!

We need stillness. In stillness comes healing of mind and body. In stillness comes the renewing of strength—"in quietness and confidence shall be your strength." In stillness we receive forgiveness for the sins of yesterday, strength for the challenge of today, and new vision for the adventure of the morrow. Only when other voices are still can we hear the voice of God. That is why it is necessary to spend a few moments alone every day listening for God to speak. He came to Elijah, not in the storm or in the wind, but in "the still small voice." At all times we may enter the chapel of our souls. There we have the silence of Cathedral Woods; there we may hear God. . . . "Be still and know that I am God."

Dear Lord, I would close the ears of my soul to the clamoring voices that cause me to doubt and fear. Speak, Lord, and command "Peace be still." And there will come to me a great calm, and in the silence I will find Thee.

15

DEDICATION

Bring them hither to me.—Matthew 14:18

... present your bodies a living sacrifice.—Romans 12:1

When we consider the starvation in our world, both physical and spiritual, the sorrow, the sin, the wretchedness, the ignorance, the misery, the wickedness, we are overwhelmed, we are crushed with a sense of inadequacy. What can *we* do? Our greatest achievements seem but a drop compared to an ocean of need. Discouragement overtakes us, and we are ready to despair. But, listen! In the story of the miracle of the feeding of the multitude Jesus, speaking of the few loaves and fishes, said, "Bring them to me." Only five small loaves and two little fishes, but in the hands of Jesus they were quite adequate to meet the need. You may have only one loaf, one small fish, only one talent or gift or capability as housewife, as mother, as businessman, as social leader or executive. Whatever you have, bring it to him and see what he will do with it. You are like one of those small loaves and fishes—inadequate, helpless. Bring yourself to him and let him take you as he did the bread; let him bless you, and break you, and *give you*. Then wonder of wonders, the physical and spiritual needs of others will be met; the people will be fed and filled. There is no limit to what our great God and Master can and will do with those who are completely yielded to him.

Dear Lord, I pray that you will take me and use me as you will. I want my life to minister to the needs of others. I would be bread—bread in your hands.

THINK

... think on these things.—Philippians 4:8

... bringing into captivity every thought to the obedience of Christ.—2 Corinthians 10:5

"Think," writes the Apostle Paul. Too often our words and acts are the result of impulse or of passing emotion rather than of intelligent thought. Public benches are filled with people who have stopped thinking altogether. They are called "the living dead." Thought shapes our lives; it is the seed of acts. Napoleon said, "I fear an idea more than an army." Thought is representative, not only of man's achievements, but of man himself, for "as he thinketh in his heart, so is he" (Prov. 23:7). That is why the Apostle Paul exhorted the young Christians of Philippi to *think aright*. He wrote: "Whatsoever things are true, honest, just, pure, lovely and of good report, if there be any virtue, any praise, *think on these things*." Thinking of truth helps one to be honest; thinking of justice will make one fair at all times and to all people. Thoughts that are pure will automatically cause one to reject impurity in action. And I am glad the Apostle spoke of loveliness! Beauty is a glorious gift of God, and thinking about it helps to beautify both character and surroundings. Also, letting the mind dwell on good report, on virtue and praise, makes it unlikely that we will think critically or condemningly of others. We can control our thoughts and make them follow paths that lead to joy, victory and power. Then, as the Apostle writes, "The God of peace shall be with you."

O Lord, my God, I thank you for the gift and power of thought. May I use it to be a co-worker with you and to create around me the beauty of life and character that you can smile upon.

SEA

... as many as received him, to them gave he the power. . . .—John 1:12

God has given us the spirit of power.—2 Timothy 1:7

Standing on the top of rocky headlands and looking out at the agitated sea, I sought to capture in my mind the movement of the waters as they were tossed to and fro by the wind. I hoped to be able to portray on canvas something of what I saw, but I soon realized that my feeble efforts would be totally inadequate. The words of Jesus came to my mind: "The wind bloweth where it listeth and thou hearest the sound thereof, but canst not tell whence it cometh, and whither it goeth: so is every one that is born of the Spirit" (John 3:8). If the power of the windswept sea so overwhelms the mind, how much more does the power of God in a human life defy understanding or description. Nonetheless we may feel it, we may know it, we may experience it, and then definition or explanation does not matter. Even as the sea in all its beauty and magnificence is real, so is the power of God. It is real, it is wonder-working, it is mighty; it changes weakness into strength and spiritual poverty into riches.

Dear Lord, I bring to you the problems of this day, and I thank you that nothing is too hard for you and that what I can never do in my own strength becomes possible when I depend on the mighty power of your Holy Spirit.

18

OTHERS

... God so loved ... .—John 3:16

... by love serve one another.—Galatians 5:13

What could he say in one word? It was Christmas, and William Booth had been told that a message cabled around the world to individual officers of his newly created Salvation Army must necessarily be limited to just one word. One word! He paced the room. There was so much that he wanted to say. The loneliest and most hard-pressed among his men must be cheered and encouraged. They must be made to know beyond shadow of a doubt that he trusted their consecration, their devotion to their vision and mission. They must be inspired. One word! And then suddenly he knew! Going to the table he took the pencil from the hand of his secretary and wrote down the word *others*. That word flashed its way around the world and into thousands of hearts. It was sufficient. It told the story—the whole story: God so loved *others* that he gave his only begotten Son; Jesus so loved *others* that he gave his life "a ransom for many." No man takes my life from me, I lay it down and I take it up again (John 10:17, 18). It was for *others* that the Holy Spirit came down on the day of Pentecost and transformed the disciples and through them millions of people into heroes of faith. The Church all over the world is continually pouring out its life for others. And did not Jesus say that his disciples should be known by their love for others? "By this shall all men know that ye are my disciples, if ye have love one to another" (John 13:35).

O Lord, may your concern and love for all men become mine. Enlarge my heart and understanding. Help me to live for others.

LIGHT

God is light, and in him is no darkness at all.—1 John 1:5

When I sit in darkness, the Lord shall be a light unto me.—Micah 7:8

Judas was not with them when Jesus and his disciples stood and sang a hymn after the Last Supper. He had already gone out, bent on accomplishing his evil purpose—the betrayal of his Master. And "it was night." This was in keeping with the night in his soul. Sin puts out the lights in the sky, in the churches, in the homes. Rather, light is always about us, but sin blinds our eyes. In creation God's first command was "Let there be light." That is also his first command in bringing about the *new* creation within our souls. We need light to reveal to us our need and his sufficiency. We need light to lighten us along the new way. Even in the night of sorrow and trial, we may have light within.

Somewhere I read this story: "A little child on a summer morning stood in a great cathedral. The sunlight streamed through the beautiful stained-glass windows and the figures in them of the servants of God were brilliant with color. A little later the question was asked, 'What is a saint?' and the child replied, 'A saint is a person who lets the light shine through.' "

The same God who in the beginning commanded the light to shine out of darkness, will shine in our hearts, and give us the light of the knowledge [experience] of the glory of God as revealed in the person of Christ (2 Cor. 4:6).

My Lord, I pray that you will take away darkness—darkness in my soul, darkness on my way. If there is sin in my heart obstructing your light, reveal it to me, and I will remove it. May your light flood my soul that, like Jesus, I ma. sing even on the way to the cross.

20

PRIDE

He hath scattered the proud.—Luke 1:51

. . . my soul shall weep . . . for your pride.—Jeremiah 13:17

What inconceivable fools pride makes of us. Yes, and what arrant cowards! It betrays us into committing mistakes and even wrongs; it stiffens our resistance against admitting them, justifies us at the expense of truth, and steels our wills against asking pardon. In the book *The Reason Why*, Cecil Woodham-Smith gives a striking portrayal of the stupidity of pride in one man, Lord Cardigan. That pride caused the tragic charge of the Light Brigade in the Crimean War and the needless death of England's noblest and bravest.

Pride is stupid indeed, for we have nothing that we have not received. Every gift, ability, privilege and opportunity, instead of making us proud, should only add to our sense of responsibility to God and our fellowmen and humble us through the realization of what is expected of us. Even our accomplishments are never due to ourselves alone.

Pride makes the rich possessions of mind and heart spiritually unproductive. Conversely, *humility* is the key to spiritual life, growth and achievement. His consecrated gifts added to a beautiful humility caused George Washington Carver, born of slave parents, to become one of the world's greatest scientists and spiritual leaders. Jesus said that the proud shall be abased, but the humble shall be exalted (Luke 14:11).

Dear Lord, you do not walk with the proud and the haughty. I pray that you will remove pride from me, even the pride of which I may not be aware, that I may consciously walk with you.

GOD

Great indeed . . . is the mystery of our religion.—1 Timothy 3:16 (RSV)

I am God, and not man; the Holy One in the midst of thee. . . .—Hosea 11:9

Why stumble at the mystery of God? If one accepts God at all, one must accept mystery, for God himself is the greatest of all mysteries. Were the human mind able to contain the full concept of God it would be greater than God, since the container is necessarily greater than the contained. Can a worm understand a man? No. But this does not affect the reality of man. Also, how could we worship a God whom our small minds fully comprehended? Isaiah tells us that God's ways and his thoughts are higher above ours than the heavens are above the earth.

However, we may get glimpses of God's aspects, attributes and glory even as Moses was allowed to see "his back" (Exod. 33:23). Nature is one of the mediums through which God reveals himself. In the light we have a remarkable illustration of the triune God, for though light is a *unit*, it has three distinct properties: the actinic, the luminiferous and the calorific. The *actinic*, radiant energy, cannot be seen and, thus, well represents God the Father, for "no man has seen God at any time." The *luminiferous*, light as we see and understand it, calls to mind God the Son, the visible expression of God, he who said of himself, "I am the light of the world," and "He that hath seen me hath seen the Father." And the *calorific*, heat in the light, suggests God the Holy Spirit who is the fire of the love of God in our hearts—the fire burning up the dross in us and refining the gold, the fire which came down from heaven on the day of Pentecost and transformed a small group of men and women

22

into heroes of faith that through them it might transform the world.

O God, give me a greater sense of your reality as Father, Savior and Holy Spirit whose love, salvation and quickening energy I may experience daily.

GUIDANCE

Thine ears shall hear a word . . . saying, This is the way.—Isaiah 30:21

In all thy ways acknowledge him, and he shall direct thy paths. —Proverbs 3:6

Do you believe in divine guidance? In the book *A Man Called Peter*, it is told how Peter Marshall was warned by an audible voice at night when he was two feet from a deep pit. The warning saved him from a terrible fall which might have killed him. For Elijah on the mountain, God was not in the fire or in the earthquake, but in "the still small voice." If you think that God does not speak to man, it may be that you have not listened. One has to listen to hear a "still small voice." Millions of minutes are wasted in foolishness or idle talk. Why not practice using otherwise wasted moments to listen to the voice of God in your soul that you may receive guidance? This will prove a most rewarding habit, especially if you determine not only to listen but to obey. "Religion cannot be separated from life. The source of power is to be found within—the attention must be turned inwards in stillness. We must make the conscious effort to come in touch with the Father of our spirits if our souls are to be enlightened, our love kindled, and our wills braced to fulfill the purposes of God" (Quaker Discipline).

Dear God, I thank you that you have not left me to grope my way in the dark. I thank you for the guidance you are ready to give me and I now ask for the knowledge of your will in my particular problem.

MEN

Be thou strong therefore, and shew thyself a man.—1 Kings 2:2
. . . by my God have I leaped over a wall.—Psalm 18:29

Do not act like a baby! Do not pity and indulge yourself. Life calls for heroes. The Apostle Paul wrote to the early Christians, "Quit you like men," and they did. Who is not moved when reading of their going out to meet death in the arena with a song on their lips?

There is no obstacle, no difficulty that cannot be either removed or overcome if we go ahead with courage and with faith in God. Faith, "even small as a mustard seed," Jesus said, "will cause a mountain to be cast into the sea." Perhaps there is a mountain now facing you. Go on, just quietly go on, not looking to tomorrow, keeping your eyes on God, and the mountain will retreat as you advance; it may even disappear. How often do we read in the Scriptures such words as: "Be of good courage," "He shall strengthen thine heart," "Fight the good fight," "Be strong in the Lord." And we have Paul's glorious testimony: "When Christ strengthens me I am able for anything—anything."

Dear Master, deliver me from self-pity. Make me ashamed of weakness. May I press on even though my heart is heavy, even though I do not see my way. Give me the faith that opens before me the deep sea of the unknown, that removes mountains of difficulty. Grant me courage, and I will see miracles of your deliverance.

FREEDOM

Stand fast therefore in the liberty wherewith Christ hath made us free.—Galatians 5:1

If the Son therefore shall make you free, ye shall be free indeed.—John 8:36

What could be said to these men in the striped garments of convicts in a penitentiary? What utterance could reach them in the depth of their sullenness and despair, their resentment and bitterness, their evil thinking and vengefulness? "Give me the right words," I prayed, and all at once I knew! I must speak to them of freedom. Freedom in prison? Yes. "Every one of you," I told them, "can be a free man—free in spirit. No one is truly imprisoned except by himself." I reminded them of the words of the Apostle that he who commits sin is the slave of sin. I told them of good men who had been happy in chains because their spirits were free. "Your own soul is your castle; no one can imprison your spirit. A physically free man may be the miserable prisoner of his evil passions, and a prisoner may be gloriously free with the liberty of the sons of God. Your soul can soar into the presence of God and there find peace and joy, and then you will be ready for life or for death. Don't remain in chains. When your spirit is free you really live. Let God set you free."

A young convict came afterwards and thanked me. There was a light on his face.

Blessed Lord, set me free with the freedom of the spirit which neither man nor circumstance, life nor death can take from me.

GIFT

. . . it is the gift of God: not of works, lest any man should boast. —Ephesians 2:8, 9

Thanks be to God for his unspeakable gift.—2 Corinthians 9:15

"I've got it, I've got it!" cried the young French artist shaking his wife awake in the middle of the night. For a moment she thought disappointment at having his painting turned down by the French Academy had driven her husband mad. But he was radiant, and with feverish haste he rose, gathered his tools —canvas, brushes, oils—and began to work. For weeks she dared not disturb him. On tiptoe she would bring his meals, often coming later to find them untouched. But this time, when again presented, his work found acceptance. That memorable night his new painting had been born whole and complete in his mind, but it had remained for him to work it out on canvas —carefully, patiently, day by day.

Like the picture in the artist's mind, our salvation is a *gift* from God. By faith we receive it whole and complete because of Christ's cross, and we *know* we have it. But from that moment we must work it out in our daily living, patiently, faithfully and carefully as the young artist worked out his painting on canvas. "Work out your own salvation with anxious care. Remember it is God who is at work within you enabling you both to will and to do" (Phil. 2:12, 13).

I thank you, O Christ, for the gift of salvation. May I prove to the world its reality by working it out daily in every part of my life, knowing that it is you who are working in me to will and to do your good pleasure.

CIRCUMSTANCES

... every one's bands were loosed.—Acts 16:26

And now my head shall be lifted up above my enemies round about me ... I will sing.—Psalm 27:6 (RSV)

After World War II how tragic and pathetic were the ruins of Greek villages! The streets were lined with houses without roofs, doors or windows. Often whole families slept on the ground. One might see a few white marble slabs and columns showing where a church once stood. And all of this destruction was caused by four successive wars in which the Greeks unhesitatingly sacrificed all for freedom. (Incidentally, their heroism saved the rest of the free world.)

In one of those villages I was startled by the continuous singing of a girl. Even into the night her voice rose, pure and clear as a bird's. Her singing imparted to the devastation a poignant beauty, a meaning, a power to move the soul. Truly we can transform our surroundings by the spirit that is in us!

The Apostle Paul said, "I have learned in whatsoever state I am, therewith to be content." And more than content, he sang songs in the night when in prison! Then his chains were loosed and the Lord delivered him. When we sing in the night our circumstances may not change, but their chains will fall away.

O Lord my God, may I experience the triumph and joy of rising above my circumstances. Rather than become their slave, may I cause them to serve you and me. I would make melody in my heart at all times.

WEEDS

... some fell among thorns.—Matthew 13:5–8

Instead of the brier shall come up the myrtle tree.—Isaiah 55:13

Weeding a garden takes hours. It is back-breaking work and seems never-ending. But great is the reward offered by a lovely garden with gorgeous flowers growing in clean soil. Many would rather work endlessly in a garden than take the trouble to weed their souls. Spiritual weeding also seems never-ending. Faults that we think have been uprooted spring up again. No wonder the Apostle James writes of "letting patience have her perfect work" (James 1:4), and Paul exhorts us not to be weary in well-doing (Gal. 6:9).

Weeds will probably continue to come up in our spiritual lives as long as we live, but let us continue to destroy them so that they will become less and less noticeable, and more and more people will observe in us the beautiful flowers of God's grace. However, before we pull weeds we must recognize them to be such. Our first act in spiritual weeding is to acknowledge our faults to God and also to others. "Confess your faults one to another," writes the Apostle James, "and pray for one another" (James 5:16). The next essential is perseverance. Let every day be the beginning of a new life. Forgetting the weeds that were pulled yesterday, let us steadfastly pull out today's weeds. And let us never forget to thank God for the flowers.

Forbid, O Lord, that I should let weeds grow unnoticed in the garden of my soul. Keep me aware of little faults lest they grow into big sins. Give me grace willingly to acknowledge and confess them, for I want my life to be your garden and to bring you joy.

29

ORANGES

I come seeking fruit on this fig tree, and find none: cut it down; why cumbereth it the ground?—Luke 13:7

Give, and it shall be given unto you; good measure, pressed down, and shaken together, and running over.—Luke 6:38

I am an orange tree. I work hard to produce. I take from the earth, the air, the sun, the dew and the rain, but that which I take I transform within myself into luscious fruit which delights the eye with its glowing beauty and feeds the hunger and quenches the thirst of man. When my fruit is ripe, I throw it out bountifully. I give to all who will take and cover the ground with my abundance. I give no matter whether my fruit is picked, admired and enjoyed, or whether it lies on the ground rotting and forgotten. I give because my joy is giving, and in giving I fulfill my destiny. What about you, O man? To give is also your destiny. Let it be your joy. Don't count the cost. Don't wait to know whether you will be appreciated. All you and I have was given to us by God; we must pass it on freely, generously, and gladly. Thus consciously or unconsciously, we enrich the world. We exist to serve—I as an orange tree, you as a man.

O Lord, do I make people glad because I am? Do I enrich others with my life? Do I bring beauty, spiritual health and strength to those who know me? This I want to do and so be like you, my Lord and Master. Save me from being a cumberer of the ground.

SPUTNIK

The nations that forget God shall be turned into hell.—Psalm 9:17

Who knows, God may yet repent and turn from his fierce anger, so that we perish not?—Jonah 3:9 (RSV)

The world will not forget the fabulous launching of the first man-made satellite. It emphasized in a dramatic way that the fruit of the tree of knowledge is both good and evil, depending on its use (Gen. 3:22). The ultimate and most decisive matters that concern mankind are those of good and evil. Even the survival of man depends on which of these qualities predominates. If in our world evil—lust for power, hatred, prejudice, fear, pride—overcomes good, mankind is doomed to destruction; if good—compassion, generosity, patience, faith, humility— overcomes evil, knowledge will become the servant of man's spiritual happiness (the only happiness that is valid) and, thus, the servant of God. Without God, as the Apostle Paul states it, man is "dead in trespasses and sins." But when the Spirit of God permeates and re-creates man's spirit, good becomes stronger than evil in him and, therefore, in his little corner of the world. Will there come a universal turning to God on man's part that righteousness, justice, mercy and truth may prevail? Or will God's judgment finally fall on a wicked world as it did in Noah's day?

Dear God, may I in some way contribute to a turning to you which shall spread throughout the world.

THORN

. . . there was given to me a thorn in the flesh, the messenger of Satan.—2 Corinthians 12:7

For my very weakness makes me strong in him.—2 Corinthians 12:10 (PHILLIPS)

You have some trial, difficulty or sorrow peculiarly your own. You need help. In his letter to the Corinthians, the Apostle Paul tells of a severe affliction which he calls his "thorn in the flesh." This "thorn" must have represented a very sore trial indeed, for he besought God three times to deliver him from it. It is good that we do not know the nature of Paul's affliction, because we might be tempted to claim that ours is worse. God did not deliver Paul. God does not always answer our prayers in the way we wish. He sees what we cannot see— the good that can come to us and to others only through our suffering. God did something better for Paul than to remove his "thorn," and he will do it for you. He said to him, "My grace is sufficient for thee: for my strength is made perfect in weakness" (2 Cor. 12:9). From that time on, Paul tells us, he gloried in trials and infirmities because they occasioned a marvelous opportunity for *proving* the sufficiency of the grace of God and the perfection of divine strength.

Dear Lord, may I experience with Paul that your strength is made perfect in my weakness, and that your grace is sufficient for all my need. At your feet, I appropriate this strength and this grace and go forward believing that I can "do all things through Christ who strengthens me."

FRUIT

I have chosen you, and ordained you, that ye should go and bring forth fruit, and that your fruit should remain.—John 15:16

The fruit of the Spirit is love, joy, peace, longsuffering, gentleness, goodness, faith, meekness, temperance. . . .—Galatians 5:22, 23

That which matters most in life is unseen, intangible, spiritual. One cannot see or handle LOVE, JOY, PEACE—no amount of money can buy them; yet without them, life is not worthwhile. Listen! The Apostle Paul wrote that love, joy and peace are *fruit*—fruit of which the root is the Spirit of God. We cannot have fruit without root. No matter how much we may want to do so, we cannot create love, joy, peace. We cannot force ourselves to forgive our enemy even though bitterness may be poisoning our life. But God's Spirit will bear in our heart the fruit of love, then forgiveness will follow naturally. All our efforts cannot create joy, but God's Spirit brings a strange and deep joy to fruition within us—a joy that the world cannot give or take away. We cannot in our own strength rise above sorrow or conquer passions which threaten to tear us apart and find peace. But God's Spirit will heal heart-wounds and will say to the storms in our soul, "peace, be still." And do not forget that God is more willing, Jesus told his disciples, to give his Spirit to those that ask him than a father is willing to give good gifts to his children. Jesus said, "Ask . . ."; ask your Heavenly Father, and you will receive the Holy Spirit. And when you have the root, you will have the fruit—love, joy, peace.

Dear Lord, I pray for your Spirit in his fullness to dwell in me. May the fruit of your Spirit abound in my life, especially love, joy and peace.

33

HIGHWAY

. . . make straight in the desert a highway for our God.—Isaiah 40:3

And an highway shall be there, and a way, and it shall be called The way of holiness; . . . wayfaring men, though fools, shall not err therein.—Isaiah 35:8

Isaiah must have understood the science of building highways. He writes, "Every valley shall be exalted, and every mountain and hill shall be made low: and the crooked shall be made straight, and the rough places plain" (Isa. 40:4). Have you ever thought of your life as a highway along which God may ride in all his splendor and power? Study the lives of those who have been God's highways, and you will see how their mountains were brought low and their valleys were filled up. Mountains of pride and ambition in the lives of Augustine and Francis of Assisi were brought low. The vision and confessions of one and the love and joy of the other filled their valleys; and along their highways countless men and women met God. The valley of humiliation, disappointment and loneliness in the imprisoned life of John Bunyan was exalted and filled with vision and faith and became the highway along which *Pilgrim's Progress* brought its message to the world. The crooked and rough places in the life of a modern-day criminal were made straight and plain, and he became Starr Daily whose spoken and written messages were truly a highway along which God walked into millions of lives. Any life, however rough, rude and crooked, may through God's workmanship become the highway along which he will walk.

My dear Lord, I would that my life might be a highway along which others may meet you. Bring down every high mountain of self-esteem and bring up every valley of discouragement. Help me to straighten every crooked place. May no one get confused or lost because he is following me. Keep me straight in the big and little concerns of life.

CHILD

Verily I say unto you, Whosoever shall not receive the kingdom of God as a little child, he shall not enter therein.—Mark 10:15

... of such is the kingdom of heaven.—Matthew 19:14

Jesus said we must be as little children if we would enter the Kingdom of Heaven. What did he mean, for we know that children are often naughty? Evidently Jesus had in mind certain characteristics shared by all children. Little children are trustful; they allow their parents to take them here and there without being tormented by doubts and fears. Shall we not trust our Heavenly Father to lead us, he who knows the end from the beginning? Little children respond to love and give love spontaneously. God's love is all about us and seeks to enter and saturate our being. Why not respond to this love and let it flow into us and out of us to others? (The Apostle John called the early Christians "little children" and exhorted them to love one another.) Also little children have pure hearts. Impurity is destructive to health of soul and body and to mental peace. Let us ask our Lord to cleanse our hearts and minds (our emotions and thoughts), and to *keep* them clean by his Holy Spirit dwelling in us. Thus, shall we be as little children and enter the Kingdom of Heaven.

Dear Lord, give me the heart of a child in simplicity, obedience, trust and love. Cleanse my thoughts, drive away my fears. I commit my life with all its problems to your fatherly care.

FATHER

... your Father.—Matthew 7:11

One God and father of all.—Ephesians 4:6

A minister visiting an orphanage was asked not to refer to God as "Father" in his talk to the children. The explanation was that the children came from broken homes and that most of them had delinquent fathers. How tragic! Father is a noble name which should always suggest love, strength and protection. We greatly need to know God as Father—"our Father."

> O take my hand, my Father,
> Lead Thou me on:
> Lord, not my will but rather
> May Thine be done.
> One step alone I dare not
> Without Thee go:
> When Thou dost lead I care not
> My way to know.
>
> Keep in Thy will abiding
> My wayward heart:
> There ever gladly hiding,
> Its fears depart.
> Thyself to me revealing
> So kind and just,
> I ask not sight or feeling,
> But blindly trust.
>
> When darkness is the deepest,
> The path unknown,
> Thy watch Thou ever keepest,
> Thou faithful One.
> What matters then my weakness,
> Since I am Thine?
> Thy strength, Thy love, Thy meekness,
> Yes, all is mine.
> —Arthur Sidney Booth-Clibborn
> (father of the Author)

FAITH

I

Only faith can . . . prove the existence of the realities that at present remain unseen.—Hebrews 11:1 (JERUSALEM BIBLE)

If ye have faith as a grain of mustard seed . . . nothing shall be impossible to you.—Matthew 17:20

Let us not mistake belief for faith. Belief is in the mind; faith fills the whole being. Belief is the product of your own thinking; faith is inspired by its object—God. A minister called on a sick woman and asked her what she believed. She answered, "You will find my beliefs in that drawer, pastor." He looked and found nothing. "Oh, they were carefully filed! I must have lost them." Her beliefs were put away in a drawer—they meant nothing to her and had no bearing on her life. Faith is not, as some think, to be obtained through much struggle and agony. It is received from God just as the earth receives rain, and the flowers receive sunshine. And faith lives and grows by action. No matter how small your faith is, use it, share it, and go forward.

The father of the poor boy out of whom Jesus cast the evil spirit realized that his faith was weak, but he used the little he had and at the same time cried out for more: "Lord, I believe; help thou mine unbelief" (Mark 9:24). And his boy was delivered.

God never blesses spiritual slothfulness. In the spiritual as in the physical, exercise prevents atrophy. Exercise faith and it will grow stronger. Expect more and more from God and fit your actions to your faith. That is what the man with the withered hand did. He stretched out his hand in obedience to the command of Jesus; he made the effort, and his hand was healed. And remember the object of our faith is not something —a creed, a church—but *someone.* Paul did not say, "I know *what* I have believed," but "*whom* I have believed, and that he is able . . ." (2 Tim. 1:12).

Dear Lord, I love you. May I trust and obey you in little things that my faith may grow strong for the big things.

FAITH
II

According to your faith be it unto you.—Matthew 9:29

Without faith it is impossible to please God.—Hebrews 11:6

"Fight the good fight of faith," wrote the Apostle Paul. Faith always means a fight. Faith is not for cowards. Having faith means walking ahead in the dark night with not a glimmer of light. It means walking on a stormy sea. It means walking with great mountains looming ahead. It means singing when your heart is breaking. It means shouting, "Hallelujah," when only echoes answer you. It means asking and asking and asking like the persistent widow in the Gospels. But the promise is there: "ask and you shall receive," "walk and you will not faint," "the mountain shall be cast into the sea," "go forth weeping and you will come back rejoicing." For he is not only able, but he *does* do exceeding abundantly above all you can ask or think according to his power that works in you (Eph. 3:20).

Lord, give me faith, the faith that moves a mountain; Lord, give me faith, the faith that knows no fear; Lord, give me faith of peace and joy the fountain. Lord, give me faith.

KNOWING

Have I been so long time with you, and yet hast thou not known me . . . ?—John 14:9

If thou hadst known . . . the things which belong unto thy peace. —Luke 19:42

A dinner was given by a Dutch Baron in honor of my mother who, in those days, was head of the Salvation Army in Holland, and she was requested to bring her young children. There were five of us at the time. (Later there were ten.) At the top of the magnificent marble stairway in that stately home Mother gathered us around her: "Now you are not to say one word at the table," ("Pas un mot") she insisted. We all promised—Willie, the youngest of us, with many hugs and kisses. When seated, Mother, knowing Willie, wished he had been seated next to her that she might warn him when necessary with a surreptitious touch; but she was at the Baron's right and Willie near the foot of the table. All went well, the butler was serving the soup, when suddenly a heavenly smile illumined Willie's face, his blue eyes danced, and a high pitched voice rang out: "Ah, Maman (French was our native tongue), si j'avais su que tu étais si charmante je serais venu dans le monde il y a longtemps." ("Ah, Mother, if I had only known you were so charming I would have come into the world long ago.") The guests exploded with laughter, the icy formality was broken, and the party was a great success. When the Baron said good-bye he urged Mother to come again and said, "Please bring that little boy."

What kind of knowledge was Willie talking about? He could not know Mother as her biographer would know her. His was a knowledge of the heart, a knowledge born of love. Jesus said to the Samaritan woman: "If thou knewest the gift of God, and who it is that saith to thee, Give me to drink; *thou wouldest have asked of him"* (John 4:10). *Love* imparts true knowledge of God.

O God, may I ever seek a deeper understanding of you—knowledge of the heart rather than of the mind—the knowledge born of love.

SONG

And when they had sung an hymn.—Matthew 26:30

The sufferings of this present time are not worthy to be compared with the glory which shall be revealed in us.—Romans 8:18

Have you ever visualized Jesus singing? Why not? His whole life was a song! He himself was music—the music of God. Jesus stood with his disciples and sang. The remarkable thing is that he sang just after he had had his last supper with them and just before the agony of the Garden of Gethsemane and then—the cross! He knew he was going to die. He had told his disciples so. He also knew that before the end he was going to be betrayed by one of them and denied by another; and yet, he sang! This was victory, the very essence of it. The Apostle Paul gives us the secret when he writes: "For the joy that was set before him endured the cross, despising the shame . . ." (Heb. 12:2). Christ looked beyond—beyond the agony of the Garden, beyond the betrayal by friends, beyond the scourging and mocking, beyond the horrible death. He saw the blessing, the pardon, the deliverance, the transformation that would come to all generations through his sacrifice. And he sang! For you also, the secret of victory is to look beyond—beyond the sorrows and troubles of the moment, knowing that God has a purpose in all these things. Trust him and in the midst of your sorrows you will find a song.

O Lord, help me to turn my troubles into treasure and my sorrows into song.

HEROISM

I have seen thy tears.—Isaiah 38:5

There is a heroism far greater than that of the bandsmen who quietly played "Nearer My God to Thee" while the *Titanic* was sinking into the depths of the sea or that of the man who goes forward under fire of the enemy in war. Greater is the day by day heroism of the faithful wife of an alcoholic or of the husband whose wife has a cruel temper and a bitter tongue. Perhaps even greater is the heroism of countless others who patiently suffer in body or in spirit, not supinely, not whiningly, or resentfully, but with high courage, even joy. They may be unsung, unapplauded, unappreciated, but write these words on your heart: no sacrifice, no suffering bravely borne remains unrewarded. Sometimes the reward is inherent in the resulting development of noble character or in the change that simple goodness brings about in the character of others. But the reward comes, for it is a law—the law of God, that somehow and sometime we will reap if we faint not (Gal. 6:9).

I ask you, Lord, just for today, that you will enable me to play with courage the role in life assigned to me. Keep me from self-pity, from fear and doubt. I would trust your love and prove the sufficiency of your grace.

WOUNDS

Rejoice, inasmuch as ye are partakers of Christ's sufferings.—
1 Peter 4:13

It is now my happiness to suffer for you. This is my way of helping to complete, in my poor human flesh, the full tale of Christ's
afflictions still to be endured, for the sake of his body which is the
church.—Colossians 1:24 (NEB)

Some people must have evidence before they can believe.
They seem unable to go forward "in the dark." They must feel
solid ground under the feet of their faith. Thomas was one of
these people. And the risen Christ did not rebuke him, rather
he as much as said, "If you must have tangible evidence of my
reality, Thomas—if you must know that it is truly I and that I
am risen from the dead—come, do as you asked to do, put your
hands in my wounds" (John 20:25). His wounds were the iden-
tifying marks that Thomas had asked to see and to feel. Today
it is the same—the world asks for evidence. Churchly power
and circumstance, theological dogma, the sacraments, sermons—
these do not prove the reality of a risen Christ. It is the burning
and bleeding wounds in his body, the Church, which are the
greatest evidence that he is living. In Germany, China, Africa,
and in our own country, wherever his disciples are bravely suffering and sacrificing, their wounds speak aloud of his love and
of his passion to save men. Sermons may fall on deaf ears, but
wounds are convincing. The Christian, called upon to suffer for
Christ's sake, should carry his wounds proudly as an insigne.
Paul wrote: "I bear the marks of Jesus branded on my body"
(Gal. 6:17, NEB).

*Dear Lord, let me not resent or be ashamed of any wounds
that I bear for your sake. Why should I shun the cross when it
marked the whole of your life? Give me the grace and courage
to suffer wounds that through them others may recognize you.*

45

MARRIAGE

I

I will make a companion for him, a helper suited to his needs.—
Genesis 2:18 (LIVING BIBLE)

Be fruitful, multiply, fill the earth and conquer it.—Genesis 2:28
(JERUSALEM BIBLE)

In the story of the first "marriage" as related in the Book of
Genesis we are given its two purposes as divinely intended:
companionship—"a helpmate," and children—"be fruitful and
fill the earth." The second purpose has been accomplished as
witnessed by the world-wide population explosion. Now the human pendulum has swung to the other extreme, and with the
avoidance of children companionship is being exploited and
overemphasized. This is evidenced by group marriages and the
proliferation of unions outside wedlock. The prevention of
children has permitted intercourse to have free rein in and outside marriage, but unbridled sexual license, instead of promoting
true companionship, destroys it. Marriage was intended to control and sanctify sex and to protect companionship and children.

Monogamy is the ideal for man. This is supported by both the
Bible and experience. Jesus called sexual union outside marriage
adultery, and with few exceptions the great lovers of history desired marriage, thus confirming this as nature's way of establish-
ing and protecting their overwhelming love. Witness the Duke
of Windsor who gave up a throne rather than have "the woman
I love degraded to the position of mistress." Marriage is the only
honorable sexual union, and every self-respecting man or
woman, certainly every Christian, should endeavor to achieve
true companionship with his or her mate with the sanction of
a marriage—a companionship which is a protecting blessing to
the children and which God can smile upon.

O Lord, we need you most of all in our marriage. Give us your grace, your wisdom and guidance and most of all your love. Only then can we solve problems and overcome obstacles.

MARRIAGE

II

The two become one person.—Genesis 2:24 (LIVING BIBLE)

Conduct your married life with understanding . . . because you share together in the grace of God.—1 Peter 3:7 (NEB)

The successful marriage is *triune*—a union of spirit, soul, and body. Man's spirit is his God-contact; his soul is his world-contact; his body is his self-contact.

First must come the union of the spirit. As Paul wrote: Do not be mismated with unbelievers. For what fellowship has light with darkness, or unbelief with faith? (2 Cor. 6:14). In marriage, lovers should be one in their religion.

Next comes the union of the soul, which encompasses the mind and the emotions. The best definition of soul-love is "friend." A man and his wife should be best friends. An artist, for example, should not marry a person who lacks appreciation for his art, nor should a sports lover marry a bookworm.

Last comes the union of the body—an irresistible physical attraction between the lovers.

One cause of today's multiple divorces is that we have reversed this divine order. Couples put the body first and then the soul. The spirit comes last, if at all.

Water does not rise above its level. And if love begins on the lowest, the physical plane, it is likely to end there. Unlike a mere animal, man needs more than physical satisfaction. To endure, physical love must be nourished by soul and spirit love.

On a number of occasions a man or a woman has come to me after one of my meetings to exclaim radiantly, "I was born again while listening to you preach and simultaneously I fell in love with my wife (or husband)." The all important *spiritual* union had finally been achieved, and with it true love was born.

48

Dear Lord, for the sake of my mate in marriage and for my children's sake, help me to put you first. And if there is no spiritual union in our marriage, help me so to manifest your love that I will win my companion.

POWER

. . . power to become the sons of God.—John 1:12

But you will receive power when the Holy Spirit comes upon you.
—Acts 1:8 (NEB)

This is the age of power. The power of nuclear energy holds
our world in its thrall. It holds the secret of the healing of human
ills or of the complete destruction of human life. Power has become the god of modern man. Have we forgotten the command-
ment, "Thou shalt have no other gods before me," and the
warning, "The nations that forget God shall be cast into hell"?
Germany forgot God and worshiped power and was cast into
the Nazi hell. Russia, in sacrificing all human values to the "sys-
tem" and the attainment of world domination, became a vast
human prison. Here in America the words inscribed on our
coins, "In God We Trust," tell the world that God is our God.
But is he? Everywhere the incense of adoration is offered to the
gods of education, pleasure, money, success, so-called progress
and power. Unless there is a return to the God of our fathers,
this nation will not escape the fate of those that have been destroyed by the very "power" they worshiped. The power most
to be desired is that power which changes men's lives from
within. "As many as received him [Christ], to them gave he
power to become the sons of God" (John 1:12). To be sons of
God and to act as sons of God in these our times—this should
be the chief ambition for ourselves and for our children.

*O God of our fathers, forgive our selfish materialism. We turn
to you in repentance, for you, "our help in ages past," are still
"our hope for years to come."*

50

SHELLS

... whatsoever things are lovely.—Philippians 4:8

He hath made every thing beautiful.—Ecclesiastes 3:11

A centerpiece of flowers made with shells in their natural colors adorns the center of my table in Florida. These shells, in their countless varieties, were once inhabited in the depth of the ocean by tiny creatures who labored to make them lovely. Then they were cast on the shore by waves of the restless sea.

Each of us at times feels as though he is a shell, cast off and of little use. When dreams are dead, hopes shattered, plans gone awry, one is tempted to wonder what was the use of all the faith, the pain, the effort. But shells are gloriously beautiful; they glisten with all the radiant colors of the rainbow and adorn countless persons and homes. And likewise our dreams, fulfilled or unfulfilled, become incarnate in us, giving unusual charm and beauty to our character and leaving marks of gentleness and goodness on our faces. Hopes and plans, even though frustrated or unfulfilled, enrich our minds with wisdom and understanding, making us valuable people as fathers, mothers, husbands, wives or friends. And though our material possessions be few, we may possess a spirit that enriches and adorns some home or church. Remember the words of the Apostle: "All things work together for good to them that love God" (Rom. 8:28).

My blessed Master, I thank you that every experience of my life, sad or happy, you can turn into riches of the spirit which I may share with others. Nothing is in vain or lost when you have your way with me.

51

TREMBLING

The fear of man bringeth a snare.—Proverbs 29:25

... perfect love casteth out fear.—1 John 4:18

How paralyzing fear becomes, particularly the fear of man! There is a word in Isaiah which is a tonic for those who are tormented by the sickness of fear: "Who art thou, that thou shouldest be afraid of a man that shall die. . . . Thus saith thy Lord. . . . Behold I have taken out of thine hand the cup of trembling; . . . thou shalt no more drink it again" (Isa. 51:12, 22). The cup of trembling holds poison for the soul: No man who drinks of that cup can be or do his best for God or for his fellows. Fear is poison, it perverts judgment, destroys liberty, kills love and faith, inhibits the power to act, darkens the present, and mortgages the future. Fear hurts the soul and prevents prayer. And whom do we fear? A man that shall die? Let us tear our souls away from bondage to people whose breath is in their nostrils. Only God has the right to possess us and to control our actions. He is all wisdom and knows the end from the beginning. The cure for fear is to live courageously in the midst of and yet above men, time and circumstance—to live in eternity *now*. Let him take out of our hands the cup of trembling that we may not drink of it again, and in its stead let him give us "the cup of faith and of salvation."

Dear Lord, may I hear you say to me, "Fear not. Be of good cheer, I have overcome the world." I need the comfort, the strength, the reassurance of those blessed words.

GREEN

Whatever you eat, whatever you drink, whatever you do at all, do it for the glory of God.—1 Corinthians 10:31 (JERUSALEM BIBLE)

The green light said "Walk" and so I walked calmly across the street between two long lines of snorting, death-dealing monsters.

Do you have God's green light about smoking, drinking, and that certain sex involvement? Call it by whatever name you will—"Conscience," "Instinct," the "Holy Spirit"—that inner voice warning or guiding you is God's red or green light.

Obedience to the green light in your soul, no matter the cost, means strength, quietness and confidence, healing for body and soul, assurance of right. But to walk on in spite of God's red light means destruction by the monsters of this world. It means spiritual, and sometimes even physical, death.

Two of my friends died of cancer of the throat. Another died of emphysema. They had failed to heed God's red light warning them of the dangers of tobacco. Cities are full of young people who are destroying themselves because they do not see or do not heed God's red light.

One day my husband, before I met him, was buying a box of cigars. My brother, who was with him in the store, said to him, "Agnew, can you smoke to the glory of God?" Agnew discarded the box and never smoked again. The text from Corinthians "to the glory of God" was for him God's green light. Could it be your green light too?

Dear Lord, I want the whole of my life to be lived to your glory that it may be an inspiration and strength to my fellow-man.

CRUCIFY

. . . we hid as it were our faces from him; he was despised, and we esteemed him not.—Isaiah 53:3

. . . they crucify to themselves the Son of God afresh, and put him to an open shame.—Hebrews 6:6

One morning my little grandson announced: "Where do you think I went last night? I went to heaven." "And what did you do there, David?" "I took all the nails out of the hands and feet of Jesus, so he won't suffer any more pain." The words in the sixth chapter of the Epistle to the Hebrews came to my mind: "They crucify to themselves the Son of God afresh, and put him to an open shame." When we are children, and our hearts are tender, we hate to think of the sufferings of Jesus. But as we grow older we crucify him again and again by our willfulness, our pride, or unkindness. And when we crucify him, we hurt our own souls; we crucify the best and the highest that is in us. Sometimes it is just our indifference that crucifies him.

Someone wrote a poem about Jesus on the streets of a modern city, forgotten in the cold and rainy night, and described him as calling for Calvary. The active hatred he experienced on the cross was easier to bear than just complete indifference and neglect. What a lovely thought that by our love, our devotion and humble service to our fellows, we, like David, may draw the nails out of his hands and feet.

Dear Lord, I will not cause you to suffer by my indifference, neglect or sin. I love you and want to love you more, that my life may bring you joy.

OBEDIENCE

Whatsoever he saith unto you, do it.—John 2:5

Often we associate obedience with children, forgetting that obedience is basic to all life and progress. Sickness and death are consequences of disobedience to the laws of health. In order to fulfill his mission in space, John Glenn gave the minutest obedience to the laws, rules and regulations governing his space ship. There would be no progress in business or in the arts and sciences without obedience.

The spiritual life is no exception. Our salvation depends on obedience. God is the author of salvation to them that obey him. After all, we are children—children of God, and as such we must give our Father in heaven absolute obedience. Otherwise we grieve his Spirit, lose his presence and his guidance, and incur the greatest loss and grief to our souls.

My conversion as a child and the whole of my life's ministry as an evangelist resulted from my having, when only six years old, obeyed the inner "still, small voice." Since that time I have had a wholesome fear of disobeying the Holy Spirit. He may speak once, maybe twice, but God says, "My Spirit shall not always strive with man." The discipline of immediate, unquestioning obedience strengthens the sinews of faith and has resulted in the greatest spiritual achievements in history which are illustrated in the lives of St. Francis, Catherine of Sienna, John Wesley, Martin Luther, William Booth and countless others. Jesus even put obedience before doctrine. "They that will to do his will shall know of the doctrine." Write that letter of forgiveness today. Be reconciled to the friend that you have alienated. "Whatsoever he saith unto you, do it." And do it NOW!

Dear Lord, I need your grace that I may obey you whatever the cost. I will to do your will, and I now receive the help of your Holy Spirit that enables me to do so.

MAGDALENE

Seest thou this woman?—Luke 7:44

Her sins, which are many, are forgiven; for she loved much.—
Luke 7:47

She was a sinner. She probably spent all her money, perhaps
even sold her jewels, that she might purchase a costly alabaster
cruse of perfume which she broke over the feet of Jesus. Why
not, if this recklessly generous gesture told him what her lips
could never express—her grief over her sins, her repentance, her
love, her deep gratitude for the light and hope he had brought?
It would be worth every sacrifice. She knew the law of Moses.
Simon, the host of the feast, had the right to have her dragged
out and stoned to death. So be it. If this was to be the last act
of her life, it must be one worthy of Jesus and of what he had
done for her.

When the great moment came and she was at his feet, she
could not speak, but her tears were eloquent, as were the kisses
she pressed on those weary feet, wiping them with her hair. And
Jesus understood. His presence protected her. "How can he be
a prophet," Simon thought, "since he does not seem to know
what kind of woman it is who touches him?" But it was Simon
who did not know. Jesus knew. In his eyes she was a repentant
daughter, a lady of gracious manners, a soul redeemed and made
pure.

And she, Magdalene, was the first to behold him after his
resurrection. Furthermore, it was Jesus himself who sent her to
tell his disciples that he was risen from the dead. Since this was
the consummation of the "good news" (Rom. 4:25), she was
really the first one to preach the Gospel—and that to his own
disciples. "Where sin abounded, grace did much more abound."

56

Dear Lord, I belong where the Magdalene was—at your feet in repentance, love and surrender. Nothing that I may sacrifice, nothing that I may give to you of my time or possessions can worthily express my gratitude for your redeeming and transforming love. May I never forget what I might be were it not for your grace.

VISION

For God . . . hath shined in our hearts, to give the light . . . of the glory of God in the face of Jesus Christ.—2 Corinthians 4:6

Where there is no vision, the people perish.—Proverbs 29:18

It happened in a southern city on a Sunday morning. A man was on his way to an appointment for an immoral purpose. As he passed a church, the announcement that a woman was to preach arrested him and he decided to enter. He was instantly gripped by my message on the text, "Sir, we would see Jesus"— the request of the Greeks to Philip when they came to Jerusalem for the feast (John 12:21).

In this man's words: "When I left the church I was reeling like a drunken man and saying over and over to myself, 'I have seen Jesus, I have seen Jesus.'" After walking some distance he came to himself and remembered what he had been about to do that morning. The thought was repugnant to him. However, he kept his appointment that he might witness to this woman of his conversion. Later he studied for the Presbyterian ministry, was ordained and became an effective minister of Christ. When we see Jesus our souls are filled with a deep longing to be like him, and we naturally turn away with loathing from that which is evil. Best of all when we see Jesus there is born in us the faith that he is able to change us into his own likeness. It happened to this man. It can happen to you!

Lord Jesus, I want to see you with my spiritual eyes: I want to catch the vision of your beauty, your glory, your love and purity and live thereafter in the transforming power of that vision.

EAGLE

They shall mount up with wings as eagles.—Isaiah 40:31

. . . thy youth is renewed like the eagle's.—Psalm 103:5

"They that wait upon the Lord," writes Isaiah, "shall renew their strength: they shall mount up with wings as eagles." The prophet goes on to write about running and not wearying, about walking and not fainting, but let us stop with the eagle. Consider that majestic bird—the ease and power with which it takes off and soars. Even in a tempest it is not afraid: it lives in the heights and its eye pierces the distance. Yes, we shall mount up like eagles *if* we wait on God. We shall mount up on the twin wings of faith and courage into the upper atmosphere of spiritual peace and confidence. But to soar, the eagle must be free. No amount of prayer will enable us to rise above our difficulties, sorrows and circumstances, if we are chained to earth by sin.

In the midst of winter an eagle spied a lamb in the snow. It swooped down and fastened its talons in the lamb's body and began devouring it. When at last it was ready to fly, behold, one of its wings was frozen to the earth. Vainly it struggled to free itself. Later it was found dead. Jesus said, "If thy hand cause thee to sin, cut it off." Though it may seem like cutting out your own heart to give up that idol—that beautiful and beloved sin— you must do it if you are not to be destroyed but instead be free and mount up as an eagle.

Lord, I want to fly; I want to rise into the pure atmosphere of your presence and love. I desire this more than anything. Reveal to me any sin that binds me to earth for I would say with the hymnist, "The dearest idol I have known, Whate'er that idol be, Help me to tear it from Thy throne, And worship only Thee."

CONTACT

I will therefore that men pray every where. . . .—2 Timothy 2:8

. . . in every thing by prayer and supplication with thanksgiving let your requests be made known unto God.—Philippians 4:6

Prayer is an act of worship; it is also a science and an art. It is an act of worship because, through prayer, man touches God, and God touches man. It is a science because it is subject to certain spiritual laws of cause and effect. It is an art because it is the medium for God's revelation to us of the greatest beauty—the beauty of holiness (goodness)—and for the attainment of that beauty by man's soul. Countless books have been written on the subject of prayer, but to me one little word describes it: *contact*. Electricity is all around us, but for darkness to be dispelled by light we press a little button, and immediately we establish contact between the electric bulb and the unseen powerhouse far away. And lo, there is light! When we, through prayer, establish contact with God, his love, his light and his power flow into us and through us to others.

Prayer is like a spiritual "walkie-talkie"—we may tune in and tune out. Even more important than talking to God is to let him talk to us. God will speak to us if we will listen. Traveling on the highway, facing a problem in the office, doing housework—at any time, in any place, a cry from the heart, even just a turning of the mind to him as the flower turns to the sun, brings a quick answer in renewed understanding, strength and courage. Why don't you try it now? At this very moment you may be in great need. Whoever you are, wherever you are —PRAY! Prayer can change your whole life, as it has changed the life of thousands.

O God my Father, there is no one to whom I may turn, and I seem to have reached "a dead end." My heart is heavy, and my spirit is weary. May I find relief and comfort in prayer, for you have promised to hear and to help me.

WISDOM

The fear of the Lord is the beginning of wisdom.—Psalm 111:10

Happy is the man that findeth wisdom, and the man that getteth understanding.—Proverbs 3:13

Human beings have perfect freedom in casting their moral votes. Every day we make decisions, and if these are not on the side of right, they are wrong. There is no neutral ground. That is why the Christian life is not for cowards. We can betray and deny our Lord by silence as well as by words or actions. How important then for us to know what is right. Sometimes questions arise and situations confront us that defy our best wisdom. We do not know what is the decision we should make or the next step we should take. But we are not left without help. Our Lord is not a dictator but a friend and a counselor. He will reason with us, advise us and help us to make the right decisions and to *stick by them!* But we must come to him with a sincere and humble spirit. "If any of you lack wisdom," writes the Apostle James, "let him ask of God . . . and it shall be given him. But let him ask in faith, nothing wavering: for he that wavereth is like a wave of the sea driven with the wind and tossed. For let not that man think that he shall receive anything of the Lord" (James 1:5–7).

O Lord, give me wisdom lest I make mistakes that hurt others and dishonor you. In faith I ask, in faith I receive, and in faith I go forward to do that which is right in your eyes.

EMPTY

... and the last state of that man is worse than the first.—Matthew 12:45

And we are his [Christ's] house. . . .—Hebrews 3:5–6 (RSV)

Jesus tells the story of the evil spirit who, when he returned to the house from which he had been driven, found it empty, swept and garnished. And he said, "I will go back into my house." Had the house been occupied he would not have been able to say "my house." Sweepings and garnishings of the soul of man, respectability, morality, reformation—these are not sufficient to keep out evil spirits. Lust may be cast out, but if the house is empty he may come back and bring with him pride, greed, jealousy, temper. In the spiritual life also, a vacuum does not remain such.

After hearing me preach on this parable, a church officer came to me and said, "Now I know what has been wrong with me all along. I am an empty house." He was moral, religious, and without reproach, but empty. We prayed and Christ took possession of his heart and life. He became radiant, purposeful, and effective!

Certainly sweep and decorate the house of your soul, but remember: "Behold I stand at the door and knock," says the Lord, "if any man opens the door I will come in and sup with him and he with me." He will fill your "house" with his joy and peace, his purity and power. Don't let your "house" remain empty!

Dear Lord, merely negative goodness does not satisfy either you or me. It is a delusion and a snare. I renounce my self-righteousness. Fill my house of life with your presence, for only so can it be protected from the invasion of evil.

PETER

... let him that thinketh he standeth take heed lest he fall.—1 Corinthians 10:12

"Thou art the Christ, the Son of the living God." A while later: "I know not the man; I know not what thou sayest." Can these statements about Jesus be made by the same man? Yes, in both instances it is Peter speaking—Peter who had left all to follow Jesus; Peter, one of the great three (Peter, James and John) whom Jesus took with him on special occasions. How could it be that a disciple as devoted as Peter, even to the offering of his life—"Though I should die with thee, yet will I not deny thee" (Matt. 26:35)—should suddenly and so completely disown the Master whom he so deeply loved? Three things caused Peter's fall: he was in the wrong spirit, the wrong place, and the wrong company. "Blessed is the man that walketh not in the counsel of the ungodly, nor standeth in the way of sinners, nor sitteth in the seat of the scornful" (Ps. 1:1). The retrogression is progressive. First Peter *walked* afar off when Jesus was arrested, then in Pilate's hall he *stood* with sinners, and finally he *sat* with the scornful. He had come down, down and reached bottom. He was ready for the enemy. If any saint on earth does these three things, he is sure to fall.

Dear Lord, my spirit is willing but my flesh is weak. It is so easy for me to be influenced by those with whom I mingle daily. Make me strong that I may at all times be found ready to own and honor you as my Master.

CHURCH

... ye are the temple of God.—1 Corinthians 3:16

.... God hath said, I will dwell in them, and walk in them. . . .—
2 Corinthians 6:16

It happened in a subway in East Berlin. I was attending the great *Kirchentag*, literally "Day of the Church" (Congress of Evangelical Laity) in 1951. The invisible Iron Curtain had been miraculously lifted, permitting the thousands of Christians of both western and eastern zones to intermingle. A sweet-looking girl of about seventeen, whose face was very pale, was standing close beside me in the crowded subway. I asked her for directions. At the mention of *Kirchentag* she began to weep, saying that she wanted so much to attend, but that her communist employer would not give her time off. She added, "I am one of the *verlorene Kinder* ("lost children" of the war); I do not know whether my father or mother is living, and I am alone in the world." "No, dear, not alone," I answered. "You are part of the one great Church of Christ throughout the world. I am from America but I am your sister. You have *Kirchentag* in your heart. No one can take the Church from you, because *you are the Church*. You can go into the chapel of your soul at any time and shut the door, and there join all Christians everywhere in worship and praise, and none can hinder you. And remember we are all praying for you." She smiled. Do you worship in the chapel of your soul? Unless you worship there, you worship not at all.

O God, I thank you for the freedom of worship which is mine. May public worship not cause me to forget that it is the worship in my soul that is important. And may my hands go out to clasp the hands of my Christian brothers and sisters everywhere.

65

COMMUNION

... this do in remembrance of me.—1 Corinthians 11:24

... is it not the communion of the body of Christ? For we being many are one bread, and one body: for we are all partakers of that one bread.—1 Corinthians 10:16, 17

Christians feel a deep regret and even a sense of shame that, because of differences in forms of worship, they cannot unitedly celebrate the Lord's Supper. Varying interpretations of the significance of Holy Communion should seem inconsequential in the light of the great union typified by this sacrament—union with our Lord and with all members of his Church universal. But despite different manner, method or form of partaking, and even despite differences of interpretations, Christians the world over do have this blessed sacrament in common and it is a *bond*. Most importantly, we should keep in mind that the outward celebration is but the visible testimony to an inward appropriation of Christ. Without the inner spiritual partaking of him as our divine food, the ceremonial partaking becomes an empty form—yes, it may even be a lie and a sacrilege. Conversely, when Christians sincerely partake of Christ in their hearts, no matter what the difference in ceremony, they are not only united to their Lord but also to each other. And thus, after all, there is only *one* Church.

I thank you, my Lord and my Savior, that you have given yourself to me as my spiritual food. May I partake of you, my life and my strength, and thus be identified with you and with your Church the world over.

BIRTH

... Ye must be born again.—John 3:7

Therefore if any man be in Christ, he is a new creature: old things are passed away; behold, all things are become new.—2 Corinthians 5:17

What a miracle is birth! Even as physical birth is preceded by months of the unconscious development of the child in the mother's womb, so spiritual birth is preceded by a longer or shorter time of unconscious spiritual preparation. The new birth of Paul on the road to Damascus was sudden—just a few words, "Lord, what wilt thou have me to do?"—and yet, it had its beginning long before. It may have begun while he—the young man, Saul—was guarding the clothes of those who stoned another young man—Stephen. Perhaps it began when he beheld the light in Stephen's face or when he heard him pray for his murderers. In any case, we read that immediately upon the death of Stephen, Saul was consumed with a passion to kill all Christians. Was this not evidence that he was "kicking against the goad" (Acts 8 and 9)? He himself was completely unaware of this. Therefore, when Jesus appeared to him and said: "It is hard for thee to kick against the goad," he immediately *knew* that Jesus must be God, for who else would know what he himself did not know about himself, that he had been resisting conviction? And, being honest, he surrendered. When the man Saul addressed Jesus as "Lord," the Apostle Paul was born. When we cry "Lord," in complete surrender to Christ, we too are born again.

Dear Lord, I thank you for the reality of the new birth and that you have made this experience available to all. May I know with certainty that I have been born again.

67

DOLL

... a cup of water to drink in my name.—Mark 9:41

Verily I say unto you, Inasmuch as ye have done it unto one of the least of these my brethren, ye have done it unto me.—Matthew 25:40

What could I say to bring a smile to the thin, wan face of this little barefoot refugee girl? She belonged to one of the families crowded in a great quonset hut in a refugee camp outside Berlin, and her large brown eyes were so sad as she looked up at me. "Hast du eine Puppe?" I asked. ("Do you have a doll?") She shook her head. A little girl without a doll seemed symbolic of the sorrows of refugee childhood. When I pressed the German marks into her little hand, saying, "Für eine Puppe" ("For a Doll"), her face lit up with a blissful smile. A doll to love; something that belonged to her to care for and hug to her hungry heart!

Jesus said that even a cup of water to a child would not lose its reward; no indeed, for the reward is in the giving! Only those who give can experience the truth of the words of Christ, "It is more blessed to give than to receive" (Acts 20:35). It is a truth that is learned only by experience. Look around you, look carefully, open your heart and your pocketbook to the crying need everywhere, and the joy of heaven will flood your soul.

Dear Lord, I would know the joy that comes only through selfless giving. Open my eyes and my heart to the needs of others. May I always remember how wonderfully you gave for me and to me.

DEATH

. . . to be with Christ; which is far better.—Philippians 1:23

Eye hath not seen, nor ear heard, neither have entered into the heart of man, the things which God hath prepared for them that love him.—1 Corinthians 2:9

Death for the Christian has been called "promotion." And so it is, for he is by death promoted to higher service—a service so inspired by love, so free of material care, so released from time and place, so joyous and glorious, that it can truly be called "rest." This rest in heaven does not mean idleness; it means freedom from the fret, labor, struggle and weariness that accompany earthly work. To pour in grief over the face of the dead does not seem compatible with our Christian faith. The loved-one is not there. What we see is only the shell which has been dropped. The loved-one is now a spirit, a minister of God, a flame of fire! "Who maketh his angels spirits, and his ministers a flame of fire" (Heb. 1:7). My son, killed in World War II, is not lying in the ground in faraway Guam; that is why I never asked for his body to be brought home. He is with God. What can be greater and more wonderful for your loved-ones than to be with God—*that* is heaven.

O my Father in heaven, it is when I face the fact of death that I need you most. Take my hand in yours, O Christ; make me to feel your presence and your love so that when I must walk on the dark waters, they will not overwhelm me.

TRINITY

He saw the Spirit of God descending like a dove, and lighting upon him: And lo a voice from heaven, saying, This is my beloved Son.—Matthew 3:16, 17

Blessed be God, even the Father of our Lord Jesus Christ.—2 Corinthians 1:3

I will pray the Father, and he shall give you another Comforter, . . . Even the Spirit of truth.—John 14:16, 17

The word *Trinity* is not found in the New Testament. The early Church did not feel the need of a definition of God. To the early Christians God—as Father, as Savior in Christ, as the Holy Spirit as the power in their lives—was as natural as the air they breathed. Their faith was their life. Often when reduced to dogma, the life goes out of our faith. The Trinity fulfills human needs in a most direct way: it commends itself to experience. One might say that the Trinity is a natural. Man needs God as his Father. To believe in him as just a "force" or some other "it" is completely frustrating. Who can love a "force," or desire to pray to a "force," or feel that a "force" cares for him? God is not an *it* but a *he*—"Our Father who art in heaven." Then man needs God as Savior, for he is conscious of sin and of his need for deliverance. In Christ, through his cross, God becomes our Savior. And last, man needs God as a power within him. The Holy Spirit is the indwelling God, our comforter, our guide, the divine power in us. Jesus said, "Ye shall receive power, after that the Holy Spirit is come upon you" (Acts 1:8). This happened on the day of Pentecost to ordinary men and women assembled together. They knew God as Father and as Savior and now they knew him as the Holy Spirit of power within. They were transformed and went out to transform the world.

O God, you who are my Father, I thank you that in Christ you are my Savior. May I also know you as an indwelling power, your Holy Spirit, and so become a transformed and transforming Christian.

WORDS

If any man among you seem to be religious, and bridleth not his tongue, . . . this man's religion is vain.—James 1:26

A word fitly spoken is like apples of gold in pictures of silver.—Proverbs 25:11

When she was sixteen, my youngest daughter wrote a poem the first stanza of which reads:

> Words, empty words! Like echoes from hidden vaults,
> They do not lay bare the soul. So hard and void of feeling,
> As pebbles in shallow pools! Less meaningful than silence,
> And yet at times so cruel they break and crush the heart!

Perhaps my daughter was overly pessimistic when she wrote these lines, but it remains true that we easily overestimate or underestimate the value and effect of words. How readily we can dismiss a needy person with words that cost nothing and so give ourselves a feeling of duty done, thereby deceiving only ourselves. And how quickly we can speak words that hurt and burn and wound and as quickly forget them while they remain in the hearer as a memory which festers in the soul. No wonder Jesus said we would have to give an answer for our idle speaking. Oscar Wilde wrote in the *Ballad of Reading Gaol* that we may kill "with a kiss." Yes, and we may kill with words. Conversely, words may also turn despair into hope, sorrow into joy, darkness into light. Words may destroy a soul, or they may transform a life. Let us rightly evaluate the power of words and use them respectfully and carefully.

O Lord, with the Psalmist I pray: "Set a watch before my mouth; keep the door of my lips," for I realize that "in the multitude of words there wanteth not sin." If through thoughtless words I have hurt anyone, help me quickly to ask forgiveness. May I use words carefully to lift and bless and never to hurt or destroy.

SIN

If we say that we have no sin, we deceive ourselves. . . . If we confess our sins, he is faithful and just to forgive us our sins, and to cleanse us from all unrighteousness.—1 John 1:8, 9

For he hath made him to be sin for us, who knew no sin; that we might be made the righteousness of God in him.—2 Corinthians 5:21

How can anyone say that sin is unreal? Pick up your daily newspaper and read. Here is a woman torturing her five-year-old nephew "because he did not mind me." One's immediate reaction is to say that she is a mental case: but she is not insane in the accepted sense of the word. It is true that sin is a condition of the mind, but so is goodness, and both are real. The one causes sickness—physical, emotional, mental; the other, health. The one disintegrates the personality; the other makes it whole. We were created not for sin but for holiness which is simply "wholeness." A guilty person often says, "How could I have done it? I must have been out of my mind." And in a sense, this is true. We read that when the Prodigal "came to himself" (his right mind), he said, "I will return to my father." To be in harmony with God and with his will is to be in our right mind. If sin is unreal, it is the most real "unreality" one can imagine for it causes most of the "real" suffering in the world. Would Christ have suffered and died for an unreality? His sufferings were very real and for a very real purpose: he himself told his disciples that his blood was shed for the remission of sin. Yes, sin is real but so is the remedy, for "where sin abounded, grace did much more abound" (Rom. 5:20).

O Lord, may I not think lightly of sin which cost you so much. I thank you for the way of deliverance through your cross.

STABLE

For mine eyes have seen thy salvation—Luke 2:30

. . . Christ Jesus came into the world to save sinners; of whom I am chief.—1 Timothy 1:15

The rough stones of a cave, the body heat of animals, and a manger—these were the setting for our Lord's birth. Why should Jesus have been born in a stable? The carpenter's home in Nazareth would at least have been clean; at least he would have had a cradle and baby clothes! For the answer to our question let us visualize the procession of human beings down the centuries—the great, the humble, the rich, the poor, the wise, the ignorant, the virtuous and the vile, the acclaimed and the outcasts—who have come to that stable to worship the Babe of Bethlehem. Certainly publicans and sinners would not have felt at home in the house of the Virgin and of the "just" man Joseph, whereas no one could be ill-at-ease in a stable! In a little child, God made himself as approachable as the dumb animals. Jesus was born on the level of the lowest that he might raise the lowest to the highest.

And lo! in a moment of time that stable became the most sacred spot on earth, even overshadowing a cathedral. There is not a heart so vile, so full of animal passion, so unclean, that Jesus may not be born therein and, thus, transform a stable into a holy place.

Dear Lord, change my heart that it may become a holy place in which you dwell.

CONFESS

He that covereth his sins shall not prosper: but whoso confesseth and forsaketh them shall have mercy.—Proverbs 28:13

Verily I say unto you, Except ye be converted, and become as little children, ye shall not enter into the kingdom of heaven.—Matthew 18:3

It was in Newfoundland. The children attending the children's meeting had scattered. I was leaving the church, when a little fellow came running up the hill. He stood before me panting. "Is it too late?" he asked, holding his cap in his hand. "Too late for what, dear?" I queried. "Too late for me to be converted." "No indeed, it is never too late." "Oh, I am glad! You said in the meeting that we must first confess and put things right before we come to the altar. Didn't you say that?" "I certainly did; I told you what Jesus said, 'Go first and put it right with your brother and then bring your gift to the altar.'" "Yes, and you said to do it now, didn't you?" "I did." "Well, I remembered I had stolen a gold watch and I ran out of the meeting and all the way home and got the watch from under my mattress and ran to the man it belonged to and put it in his hands and said, 'There it is. I am sorry I took it. I'll come back to explain but I am in a hurry to be converted.'" His face was anxious. "Can I be converted now?" "You are converted," I answered, "for conversion means 'to turn'—to turn away from sin and turn to Christ in faith." His face beamed. He had experienced the truth of the words: "If we confess our sins, he is faithful and just to forgive us our sins, and to cleanse us from all unrighteousness" (1 John 1:9). If we confess, *if!*

O my Lord, I confess ——— to you. Give me grace to confess now to any against whom I have sinned, and to make restitution.

LOVE

. . . the love of God is shed abroad in our hearts by the Holy Spirit.
—Romans 5:5

He that loveth not knoweth not God; for God is love.—1 John 4:8

The longing for love is one of the strongest and sometimes most painful emotions in human experience. It can become so acute that it develops into sickness. There is but one cure, and that is to give love—the little you have. Pour out love to others, utterly forgetting yourself. Remember, others need love too! In healing their wounds and in filling the vacuum in their lives, you will find your own need largely satisfied. There is no transforming power greater than that of love, especially when it is permeated with the love of God. Read over and over the thirteenth chapter of First Corinthians, the great chapter on love. Sometimes in seeking love we are in reality loving ourselves, but, "love seeketh not her own." Genuine Christian love is pure and unselfish; by the power inherent in itself, it burns up lower and unworthy passions. Bring love, comfort and joy to others and in so doing you will find these increased in your own heart and life. Jesus knowing this said, "Love your enemies, do good to those who hate you, bless those who curse you, pray for those who abuse you . . . and you will be sons of the Most High" (Luke 6:27–32, RSV).

Dear Lord, bathe my soul in your love: may it so fill my heart that there will be no room for self-love. May your love pour out of me to others, healing their wounds and blessing their lives.

STONES

. . . some fell upon stony places.—Matthew 13:5–8

. . . I will take away the stony heart . . . and I will give you an heart of flesh.—Ezekiel 36:26

At our summer cottage on a small island in Maine we have a garden that fills me with joy. Giant delphinium, scarlet phlox, varicolored lupine, monkshood, columbine, giant marigolds, roses and countless other flowers bloom in profusion. But this lovely garden was first a wilderness. Blackberry and wildrose bushes were tangled with underbrush and with grass that reached to my waist. All this had to be torn up by the roots. And most difficult of all, huge stones, even boulders, had to be dug out to get to the rich black soil which would nourish the flowers. Where there are brambles there cannot be flowers, and where there are stones there cannot be life and growth. So it is with our hearts. The wild, stubborn and rebellious underbrush of self-will and undisciplined passions must be uprooted and the stones of pride, greed and unbelief removed, if the seed of God is to reach the underlying good soil of a sincere heart and bring forth flowers of grace. Before Jesus would bring back Lazarus to life he said, "Roll away the stone." To tear away long-time growth and remove stones from our hearts and lives takes much labor and digging, sometimes sweat and tears, but the flowers and fruit of grace which result are a joy for our own souls and the souls of others.

Heavenly Father, give me the courage to roll away the stones in my heart and life—to confess to others, to make restitution, to humble myself. Help me to begin now!

POPULARITY

Woe unto you, when all men shall speak well of you!—Luke 6:26

. . . whose praise is not of men, but of God.—Romans 2:29

Popularity is a great temptation. It is all too easy for us to be trapped into saying or doing something wrong or shady because we want to stand in with the crowd, because we want to fascinate Mrs. Jones, or we don't want Mr. Smith to think us a prude, a "square" or a stuffed shirt. This attitude is not compatible with genuine Christianity. Jesus never considered whether what he did or said would please the crowd. He did it because it needed to be done; he said it because it was the truth. Flattery deceives us; it is poison to the soul. Doing right is its own reward. We would do well to keep in mind the words of Jesus, "How can ye believe, which receive honour one of another, and seek not the honour that cometh from God only?" (John 5:44).

O God, help me to be sincere at all times and to seek to please you rather than to please people. Then I will worthily serve both you and them.

FURY

. . . and he poured out the changers' money and overthrew their tables.—John 2:15

Be ye angry and sin not. . . .—Ephesians 4:26

Fury is sometimes a virtue, yes, even a necessity. It does good like medicine. Controlled, intelligent, purposeful fury! The Western peoples are given to the gentle grace of compassion, but there is great danger that our moral fiber become soft. We are threatened with the disease of moral leniency and tolerance to excess. Recently on television even murder was condoned: the sympathies of the onlookers were enlisted for the guilty by a beautiful woman who looked most pathetic as she said, "I would do anything for my child," and there the case rested.

A young woman of my acquaintance was in love with a married man. At first I nearly fell into the trap of being sympathetic. However, sympathy was just what she wanted but not what she needed. In the middle of the night I wakened suddenly and was overwhelmed with a sense of her danger and of my responsibility. I rose and wrote her a scorching letter telling her the plain, unadulterated truth. In her answer she wrote: "Your letter was a shock, but just what I needed. I seemed to awaken from a dream. I spent hours in prayer and I am completely delivered. Now it seems as though it all had never been."

Jesus drove the money-changers out of the temple with whips. Karl Barth writes that there is no wrath of God "which is anything else than the gracious burning of his love." Fury can be a great blessing on one condition: that it is born of love.

I pray, dear Lord, that I may never condone evil because of lack of moral courage. Give me the righteous anger necessary to combat sin, but help me to distinguish between the sin and the sinner, hating the one and having compassion for the other, remembering that I also may be tempted.

79

GREATNESS

... whosoever will be great among you, let him be your minister.—
Matthew 20:26

... thy gentleness hath made me great.—Psalm 18:35

"There is no color in soul" was the significant title of a leaflet given to me. That is true. Neither is there such a thing as a
superior race. This fallacy caused the abuses of Western colonialism, the crimes of Naziism perpetrated against the Jews, and
the injustices to the Blacks in America and South Africa. There
is no superior race, but there are superior people in every race—
superior for various reasons, but most of all, because of their
love for their fellowman. In the days of Jesus, the Samaritans
were counted inferior to Jews, but Jesus considered the Samaritan who ministered to the wounded man superior to the Levite
and the Pharisee who passed by on the other side. True greatness
is that of the soul. This was recognized by the English Archbishop who asked his godly cleaning woman to teach him her
secret of prayer. A spiritual revolution is going on throughout
the world. People are coming to realize the importance of the individual regardless of the color of his skin. In every race some
are "children of the devil." Jesus said to the Pharisees, "You are
children of the devil because you do his work." But in every
race there are the "children of their Father which is in heaven,"
because they love their enemies (Matt. 5:44–45), and this is the
superiority recognized by God.

*Dear Lord, remove from my heart narrow prejudices, deep-
rooted dislikes, unreasonable repulsions. So fill my heart with
love that I will overlook in my fellowman things I do not care
for and only remember that he is dear to you.*

PRISON

... a light shined in the prison. ...—Acts 12:7

... where the Spirit of the Lord is, there is freedom.—2 Corinthians 3:17 (RSV)

There are many kinds of prisons. Sometimes the prison of circumstances, of loneliness, of poverty may be just as hard to bear as that of actual walls shutting one in. When founding the Salvation Army in Switzerland, my mother, then a young woman, suffered imprisonment. Such imprisonment may prove to be, as it did with my mother, an experience of spiritual inspiration and exaltation, whereas the day by day imprisonment of the spirit will wear one down and bring nothing but darkness and defeat. Are you suffering imprisonment? Does there seem for you no way of escape? Have you lost hope and courage? Have you allowed your spirit to become prey to rebellion and bitterness, perhaps to unbelief and despair? The secret of deliverance is not found in seeking the opening of your prison doors, but rather in seeking the presence of someone else with you in your prison. While in prison mother wrote the famous hymn which begins:

Best Beloved of my soul, I am here alone with Thee,
And my prison is a heaven since Thou sharest it with me.

When the Lord shares your prison, it is no longer a prison. Your spirit is more important than your circumstances. When your spirit is delivered from bondage, your real prison doors are opened.

O God, when my soul feels the weight of any "chains," may I realize that liberty is one of Christ's greatest gifts and can be mine in spite of all hindrances. It is your will that I maintain my spiritual freedom, and by your grace I will.

CROSS

If any man will come after me, let him . . . take up his cross. . . .
—Matthew 16:24

God forbid that I should glory, save in the cross of our Lord Jesus
Christ.—Galatians 6:14

The cross is the central symbol of Christianity. It is the evidence of the love of God for all men. Its upright beam brings heaven and earth together; its outstretched arms embrace all mankind. It reveals the price of our salvation. The cross blazingly exposes all sham, all hypocrisy, all false and empty profession. The cross means reality. It spells love, mercy, pardon, sacrifice, humility, victory and power. It points the way that every Christian must go, for it is when we have abandoned ourselves to the will of God and embraced Christ's cross that we come into the riches of his kingdom. Look at the cross before you give of your substance. Look at the cross before you make an important decision. Look at the cross before you act regarding an injustice you have suffered. Look at the cross before attempting any great undertaking for the kingdom. Look at the cross when you are being highly praised. Look at the cross when you have suffered deep humiliation. Look at the cross when you are in great sorrow. Look at the cross!

Dear Lord, I bow in humility before your cross. Deliver me from pride of heart or stubbornness of will. May I be willing to share the fellowship of your sufferings that I may also experience the power of your resurrection.

UNLOVABLE

. . . pray for those who treat you with contempt.—Matthew 5:44

If I then, your Lord and Master, have washed your feet; ye also ought to wash one another's feet.—John 13:14

Is it possible to love the unlovable? During a preaching mission a woman came to see me. Quietly, with tears streaming down her face, she said, "I cannot love my husband, he has killed all love in my heart. He mocks my faith. I am crippled and cannot go out, and he had my beloved piano taken away without saying a word to me and had an organ brought in for himself. He has done his best to turn my two sons against me. How can I love him?" "It is true," I answered, "you cannot love your husband with a wifely love. And God does not expect it of you. But there is a love you may have for him—you may love him with the love of Christ who died for him. Christ can take all the bitterness and pain out of your heart and put compassion there instead." Many months later in a distant city I had news that this woman was dying. Then I received a telephone call. She had dragged herself out of bed while her husband was out. She said, "Please, dear, don't come to see me. My husband has threatened to slam the door in your face. Don't worry about me, I am all right and happy. I have learned to love him with the love of Christ and I have peace in my heart." Shortly thereafter, she went to be with her Lord. Yes, Christ makes it possible for us to love the unlovable.

O God, you who are love, have mercy on my loveless heart. I cannot make myself love the unlovable, forgive those who have wronged me, do good to those who treat me with contempt. Only you can heal the wounds inflicted by unkindness, and you can replace dislike in my heart with pity and hate with forgiveness.

DIAMOND

. . . like living stones be yourselves built into a spiritual house.—
1 Peter 2:5 (RSV)

He brought me up also out of an horrible pit, out of the miry clay.
. . .—Psalm 40:2

Have you ever thought of yourself as a living stone? Peter told the disciples of his day that they were just that—living stones built into a spiritual house. The statement is fascinating. *Stone* stands for strength and durability, while *living* would indicate movement and color. Does anything in nature suggest the union of these two seeming opposites—stone and life? Yes, the diamond; it is the strongest and most durable stone in existence, and yet it seems alive in the colors and movement of its rays of light. Carrying Peter's simile further, we might liken the Church to a temple built of diamonds—Christians—gathered from all parts of the world and placed by the builder himself into his Church! Diamonds are mined in the darkness of the earth; they are brought to the light of the sun to be cut and polished until they give back to the day their captured rays. Christians too have been brought out of darkness into light; they too need the cutting and the polishing, the daily friction of testing and trial, that they might give to the world the reflection of the beauty and glory of Christ. As in a polished diamond one sees the various colors that are in the white light of the sun, so in Christians who have been "cut and polished" by trial and suffering, one sees the red of love, the blue of purity, the gold of generosity, the beauty of all graces—rays captured from Christ who is "the light of the world."

O God, may I not resist the cutting and the polishing, because only then will my character reflect the beauty of my Lord.

WORKS

... that they may see your good works ...—Matthew 5:16

By works was faith made perfect.—James 2:22

The story is told of two men who missed a train for very different reasons. One trusted his watch but, lo, it had stopped because the works were faulty; the other had a watch that kept good time, but he did not trust it. One man had faith without works, and the other had works without faith. "Show me thy faith by thy works," writes the Apostle James, and Jesus exclaims, "Why call ye me Lord, Lord, and do not the things that I say?" Also, "Let your light so shine before men that they may see your good works, then they will glorify (believe in) your Father in heaven." In Weymouth's translation of the New Testament, *good works* are called "holy lives."

We are living in a day of rush and pressure. People have little or no time to spare for argument, or even to listen to the Church. A tortured, weary, frightened and spiritually hungry humanity is asking, "Does Christianity work—does it work in government, shop, office, home?" We must be able to answer in the affirmative. Our works—our lives—must *prove* the validity of our faith, hope and love. In the Scriptures, *dead works* (or works of the law) are good works done without the love of God as motivation, whereas *living works* are the outcome of the love of God. Living works are not the means but the result of our salvation; they are the fruit of which the grace of God in us is the root. Only these good works will follow us when we are gone (Rev. 14:13).

O Lord, may my life be such that I may hear you say to me one day, "Well done, you good and faithful servant ... enter you into the joy of your Lord."

DONKEY

... the foal of an ass.—Matthew 21:5

Blessed are the meek. . . .—Matthew 5:5

The little donkey stepped lightly that day! He must have been dimly aware that he was carrying a precious burden. The praise, the acclaim, the glory, so lavishly poured on his rider, flowed over him. And when he carried Jesus into Jerusalem we read "all the city was moved" (Matt. 21:10). Like that small donkey, any man may carry Jesus and he will find that people will be moved and situations changed. Francis of Assisi carried Jesus along the coasts of Italy, and that country was moved and the world is still moved by the influence of his life. St. Patrick carried him to the pagan people of Ireland, and they were so moved that Ireland became the first Christian country in the British Isles. Martin Luther carried him to Wittenberg, and as a result, the Reformation moved the world. William Booth carried him into the slums of London, and the Salvation Army has moved millions. To be a Jesus-carrier no eloquence is needed, no great and noble deeds. The essential requirement is humility. That is why Jesus chose a donkey. In his first letter to the Corinthians Paul writes: "God hath chosen the foolish things of the world . . . the weak things . . . the base things . . . and things which are despised . . . that no flesh should glory in his presence" (1 Cor. 1:27–29). Quietly we may carry Jesus everywhere, and the impact of his Spirit will move people. Then we will share his glory as the little donkey did. The great Palm Sunday hymn, "All Glory, laud, and honor," had a quaint final stanza that was dropped in the seventeenth century. It read like this:

> Be Thou, O Lord, the rider
> And we the little ass—
> That to God's Holy City
> Together we may pass.

Dear Lord, I would be your donkey. Grant me humility. I may not carry you in a great and public way, but may I always bring your presence, your Spirit of love and helpfulness to others wherever I go. This will be my joy and my reward.

TIME

So teach us to number our days. . . .—Psalm 90:12

. . . now is the accepted time . . . now is the day of salvation.—
2 Corinthians 6:2

What a priceless possession is time! Without it love and companionship, work and achievement are of no value. And yet time is completely beyond our control. The yesterdays are gone, the tomorrows are not yet; we have only today. No wonder the Apostle Paul twice wrote of "redeeming the time" (Eph. 5:16 and Col. 4:5). When time is used wisely, whether life is long or short, we have no regrets. Even leisure hours can be used so as to yield benefits both to us and others. It makes one shudder to think of the millions of hours fritted away in empty "pleasure," while no thought is given to brightening the lives of those who toil without gladness. Weeks, months and years are spent making cold, dead money while the rightful needs and longings of relatives, or of dependents for help, tenderness or joy are denied. When time is used in the light of eternity it bears noble fruit. It is said that, when dying, Queen Elizabeth the First cried to her doctor, "My kingdom for a moment of time." He answered, "Madam, I am not God." We cannot command time, but we can command its use. Today, *now*, and in all of the tomorrows let us invest our time in a God-guided way.

Dear Lord, help me to treasure time and use it wisely that it may be a source of joy and blessing to me, to those I love, to my community, and to my country. I pray this for Jesus' sake who gave all his time on earth to mankind.

VALUES

. . . seek ye first . . .—Matthew 6:33

For the kingdom of God is not meat and drink; but righteousness, and peace, and joy in the Holy Ghost.—Romans 14:17

Abraham Lincoln had a deep sense of dependence upon God. This was early implanted in his soul by his godly mother, Nancy Hanks Lincoln, who died when he was only nine years old. Her true sense of values is revealed in her words: "I would rather Abe learn to read the Bible than own a farm, if he can't have but one." In the light of history, how right she was. Had he owned a farm, he probably would never have become president. Instead, when the fate of a nation rested upon his shoulders, it was the knowledge of the Bible which contributed more than anything else to his wisdom, steadfastness and true greatness. The United States, yes, and the whole world, owes much to Nancy Hanks Lincoln for having instilled into her boy a right sense of values. Jesus said, "Seek ye first the kingdom of God, and his righteousness, and all these things [meaning material things] shall be added unto you." Stop and think: Are you seeking first material things—bank accounts, automobiles, television sets, lands and houses—and expecting the kingdom of God to be added to you? Is it the farm first and God last, or is it God first and the farm last?

Dear Lord, for the sake of those I love as well as for my own soul's sake, I would keep you first in my affections. May I love you more than father or mother, husband or wife, children or possessions, that in loving you well I may love others well and serve my generation.

TEARS

... I sat down and wept.—Nehemiah 1:4

... put thou my tears into thy bottle ...—Psalm 56:8

Upon hearing of the broken walls and fire-destroyed gates of his beloved Jerusalem, Nehemiah, captive in a far country and slave of a pagan king, "sat down and wept." Tears, usually thought to be a sign of weakness, in this instance were an indication of strength—the strength of Nehemiah's love for his people. It impelled him to approach the king with a request unparalleled in its boldness, and which might have cost him his life had the king suspected treason, for Nehemiah was the king's cupbearer—a position of the utmost confidence for he tasted the wine first lest it be poisoned. And it was "the sorrow of heart" in his cupbearer's face that moved the king, even before Nehemiah uttered a word, first to bid him speak and then to offer him all for which he asked, and even far more, that he might rebuild his beloved Jerusalem. Such is the power of sincere emotion. Knowing without feeling is ineffectual. (We may know the sufferings of refugees, but if we do not *feel* them, we will do nothing about it.)

Jesus did not despise emotion. Several times in the Gospels we read that he wept. But let us distinguish between emotion and emotionalism: the first is power, the second weakness. Man's redemption primarily is due, not to supreme intelligence or even wisdom, but to an emotion—love. "God so loved ... that he gave." Nehemiah wept and then rose to work. Sincere emotion almost *always results in action*. The Jerusalem whose walls and gates he rebuilt with the help of those who caught the passion of his devotion might well be called "a city built on tears." The Christian Church in Europe has been rebuilt on a foundation of tears. In his book *The Church Under the Cross*,

J. B. Phillips writes, "There is no such thing as Christianity without tears."

Dear Christ, move my heart with the passion of your heart. May I grieve over my coldness and lack of deep devotion. May I love you so truly that my love may find expression in the daily acts of my life.

PROOF

. . . go thy way, show thyself. . . .—Matthew 8:4

Wherefore shew ye . . . the proof of your love. . . .—2 Corinthians 8:24

I met a man on the street who said, "Show me! You say there is a God—do you know him? You say that Christ is a Savior—has he saved you from the love of money, from lust, from bad temper? You say that the Bible is the Word of God—is it a guide for you in your daily life, in your home and business? Wherein are you different from others?"

A salesman came to my home to sell an electric carpet sweeper. I was busy, but he was smart—he stuck his foot in the door. "Just a moment, Madam," he said, "I want to show you something." While he spoke his hands moved rapidly. To my horror he suddenly dumped a lot of dirt on my rug. But before I could protest, with a swift motion he swept up all the dirt, and then to my confusion I saw that the only part of the rug which was really clean was the part he had swept. I bought the vacuum cleaner! Jesus justified the world in wanting to see. He said, "Let your light so shine before men, that they may see your good works, and glorify your Father which is in heaven" (Matt. 5:16).

O Christ, help me to show by my daily conduct the greatness of your saving grace, the glory of your truth, the inspiration of your love, that others may come to believe in you because they have seen you in me.

BREAD

I am the bread of life.—John 6:35

. . . this mystery . . . which is Christ in you, the hope of glory.—
Colossians 1:27

Jesus said, "I am the living bread . . . if any man eat of this bread, he shall live for ever" (John 6:51). What do the words *eat of this bread* mean? Are they translatable into everyday experience? Let me illustrate. A man may eloquently expound to me the virtues of whole wheat bread but may still leave my home hungry. My little granddaughter snatches a piece of bread and eats it. She does not need to "understand" the bread to be fed by it. The one merely "believes" in the bread; the other receives it. The Apostle John put it very clearly when he wrote: "As many as received him, to them gave he power to become the sons of God." To believe in Christ with the mind is not enough; it is necessary to our spiritual health that we receive him by faith—accept his love, his power, into our very being. It is this appropriation which transforms. There is a faith that is dead—"Faith without works is dead" (James 2:20). Our faith is *living* when we spiritually feed on Christ in our hearts, thus making him part of us and we part of him. Also let us keep in mind that undigested bread does not nourish. Christ, God's bread, must be assimilated daily by prayer, meditation, spiritual contemplation (which is possible even in the busiest life) and the *practice* of his words. Nothing short of this daily appropriation can enable us to stand the tests of living victoriously in an unbelieving and wicked world.

O my Lord, I take you as my spiritual sustenance, that by the strength of your life I may be able to conquer all things by

CROWDS

But when he saw the multitudes, he was moved with compassion.—
Matthew 9:36

. . . the people pressed upon him to hear the word of God.—Luke
5:1

Crowds possess power that can be used for good or for evil.
Thousands of clenched fists, lifted threateningly, have shown us
the fearful might and deadly miasma of massed, militant godless-
ness. But that godlessness can be successfully opposed. In the
Olympic Stadium in Berlin during the 1951 Kirchentag Congress
of Evangelical Laity, I was one of the three hundred thousand
Christians who stood and repeated the great Christian creed, "Ich
glaube an Gott dem Vater" (I believe in God the Father). At
Soldier Field in Chicago during the Second Assembly of the
World Council of Churches in 1954, one hundred and fifty
thousand sang with one voice, "A Mighty Fortress Is Our God."
In Billy Graham's meetings across the world millions have proclaimed their allegiance to Christ. In each of these instances a
tremendous wave of faith and love has started on its way. It
crosses every national border and its tiny wave-children continue spreading until they touch countless hearts. No one better
than Jesus recognized the dignity of every individual—witness
his special ministry to the Samaritan woman and to Nicodemus.
But no one better than he appraised the significance of crowds.
To him they were as sheep without a shepherd, needing to be
loved and led. It is high time that Christ's followers realize that
unless Christianity reaches the masses, the deadly forces of god-
less secularism and materialism will. Let us close our ranks no
matter what our denominational name, and let us as Christians
make a concerted effort to reach the masses with the love of
Christ.

Crowds to you, dear Lord, were not to be exploited, com-manded, or driven. They were people, human beings infinitely dear to your heart and with infinite possibilities for evil or for good. May I too think of the multitudes in that way, as many individuals needing love, needing you.

RACE

And who is my neighbour?—Luke 10:29

The Lord seeth not as man seeth; for man looketh on the outward appearance, but the Lord looketh on the heart.—1 Samuel 16:7

There is no getting around it: every honest person knows that genuine Christianity requires that he be a true brother to his fellowman no matter what that man's race, color or creed. Read the story of Peter and Cornelius in the Book of Acts. Peter had to overcome strong, inbred, emotional prejudices against the Gentiles. To him they were not only inferior, but "unclean." Three times the Lord rebuked him in a vision. Animals pronounced "unclean" by Hebrew law were let down in a sheet and the command given, "Rise and eat." And then came a knock at the door and the request to go to the house of Cornelius a Gentile. He went and was utterly surprised and quite overcome by the nobility of the very man he had despised, and he exclaimed: "Of a truth I perceive that God is no respecter of persons." If God is not, how preposterous for us to be! It is not written, "According to his background, his nation, the color of his skin, his long hair or the beads around his neck, so is a man," but, "As a man thinketh in his heart, so is he." We in America will never fully command our own self-respect, let alone the respect of other nations, until we have conquered our racial and personal prejudices and have translated into our national and individual actions the glorious truth of man's equality as expressed in the Scriptures and, incidentally, in our own Declaration of Independence.

O Master, you who in divine humility washed the feet of your disciples, deliver me from racial pride, and melt all my prejudices in the fires of your divine love. Only by doing so may I influence my fellowman for good.

96

WORD

... the word of life. ... Philippians 2:16
... the word of truth. ... Colossians 1:5
But his word was in my heart as a burning fire.—Jeremiah 20:9

Man's words weary and confuse us; we cannot trust them for guidance and help. We need the Word of God as given to us by prophets and apostles, by Christ himself in the Scriptures, and whispered in our hearts by the Holy Spirit. God's Word is sure and strong. Jesus was hungry after having fasted forty days in the wilderness, and he was challenged by Satan to change stones into bread to prove his deity. Had he performed this miracle, he would have given nothing to the world, whereas his answer to Satan forever gave the lie to a merely materialistic concept of man, and at the same time proclaimed the supreme truth, never more needed than today, that man is spiritually dependent on God's Word. Jesus' answer was: "Man shall not live by bread alone, but by every word that proceeds from the mouth of God" (Matt. 4:4, RSV).

> Man's nature calls for food divine,
> For he is more than flesh and bone.
> He knows a discontent sublime;
> Man cannot live by bread alone.

Dear Heavenly Father, create in me a deep hunger for your word of wisdom, power and love which will satisfy my spiritual needs. May I seek to know it and gladly receive it into my heart.

RECOMPENSE

Surely the wrath of man shall praise thee.—Psalm 76:10

And let us not be weary in well doing: for in due season we shall reap, if we faint not.—Galatians 6:9

When sixteen years old he had been carried off from Scotland by a band of Irish marauders who found nothing better to do for their sensitive young slave than to tend their flocks. But the suffering, the loneliness endured by Succat, later named Patrick, resulted in his being converted to Christianity. Meanwhile he learned the language of his captors. When twenty-two he escaped to France. There he procured an education and at thirty-six was ordained to the priesthood. And then what happened? He returned to Ireland and to the people who had enslaved him, and he preached the gospel to them in their own language. Peasants and chiefs alike listened to him and were converted by the thousands. This rough people loved their spiritual father and adopted him as their patron saint.

We are reminded of another young captive—Joseph in the Old Testament, who became the benefactor of those who enslaved him; of a herdsman—Moses, who became the deliverer of a people who had exiled him; of a young shepherd—David, who played his harp for the king who hated him and later himself became king; and of a converted submarine captain—Martin Niemoeller, who when released from a concentration camp ministered to the people whose leader, Hitler, had imprisoned him. In each instance the evil intended was turned into good. God can cause the evil in your life to turn into good—if you let him.

Dear Lord, help me to believe that even my mistakes, yes, even my sins, if confessed and repented of, and my sorrows, heartbreaking as they are, may be turned by you into good and blessing for me and for others. I rejoice at the thought that nothing need be lost: everything in my life you can turn into gain.

BRIGAND

... do works meet for repentance.—Acts 26: 20

If we confess our sins, he is faithful and just to forgive us our sins, and to cleanse us from all unrighteousness.—1 John 1:9

It was in southern France in the days when, as a young woman, my mother, eldest daughter of William Booth, was pioneering the work of the Salvation Army. One early morning there was a knock on the door. When opened a giant of a man, shaggy and fierce-looking, filled the entrance. He was a mountain bandit. "On m'a dit que Jésus était ici" ("It was told me that Jesus is here"), he said, "and I want to meet him. But wait—." And with that the man opened his sack and brought out gold watches, jewels and other valuables. "See, I am a brigand, but I don't want to be one any more; I want to be good. And now may I see Jesus?" It was with joy that my mother told this man of Christ and his power to deliver from sin. Though ignorant, this poor man knew that he could not hold to sin and be accepted by God. "They will not frame their doings," cried the prophet, "to turn unto their God" (Hos. 5:4). The proof of sincerity in our spiritual quest is to bring our "doings" into line with God's will. In the majority of cases where intellectual doubts are claimed as a hindrance to faith, the real reason is some treasured sin. "If any man will do his will, he shall know of the doctrine" (John 7:17). Obedience comes first, knowledge afterwards.

Show me, Lord, whether there be anything in my heart and life of which you disapprove, and give me grace for immediate action in putting it away.

OVERCOMER

But thanks be to God, which giveth us the victory. . . .—1 Corinthians 15:57

Be not overcome of evil, but overcome evil with good.—Romans 12:21

Seven times in the Book of Revelation (and seven is "the perfect number") a promise is made "to him that overcometh" (Rev. 2:7, 11, 17, 26 and 3:5, 12, 21). How appropriate that the last book of the Bible should emphasize *victory*. The Christian life is a spiritual warfare and what is the object of war if it is not victory? Jesus said, "I have overcome the world," and through him, the great overcomer, we too become overcomers. Of the above mentioned promises, the one I love most reads: "He that overcometh will I make a pillar in the temple of my God, and he shall go no more out" (Rev. 3:12). Looking up in a great cathedral who is not profoundly moved by the sight of the majestic pillars bearing the noble edifice on their shoulders? A pillar in the house of God. The reward of the overcomer lies in being honored with bearing the Church of God on his shoulders. And "he shall go no more out." The overcomer is on the inside forever—on the inside of God's house, his kingdom, his holy temple.

O God, you are my God, and I am your servant. By your grace may I prove to be an overcomer in my personal life, in my public life, in all my relationships, that so I may be a strength to your Church and bring glory to your name.

ABUNDANTLY

... exceeding abundantly. ...—Ephesians 3:20

Call unto me, and I will answer thee, and shew thee great and mighty things, which thou knowest not.—Jeremiah 33:3

In the twentieth and twenty-first verses of the third chapter of Paul's letter to the Ephesians he writes: "Unto him that is able to do exceeding abundantly above all that we ask or think, according to the power that worketh in us, unto him be glory in the church." I love the majestic march of the words in the King James translation: "exceeding abundantly above." It is about God that Paul is writing—God who made the heavens and the earth, God with whom "nothing is impossible." When people truly believe in God, wonders happen. Not only is he able to do what we ask or think but *exceeding abundantly above* what we ask or think. This faith is no cult, no fanaticism; it is just simple Christianity. On one occasion I awakened early in the morning with those words ringing in my mind. I was suffering from typhoid fever and I began to pray, "Lord, let thy power work within me *now*." Over and over I repeated this prayer and became conscious of receiving the healing power of God in my body. When the doctor came, my temperature was normal. It is even more wonderful to witness the power of God in a spiritual victory. "Only believe," said Jesus to Martha, whose brother Lazarus had been dead four days, "and thou shalt see the glory of God," and Lazarus was raised to life.

Dear Lord, forgive me for so often limiting your power by my unbelief. There is so much for which I am not able, but you are able. Give me the faith that brings miracles to pass in my life and in the lives of others.

FIGS

... the fig tree which thou cursedst. ... .—Mark 11:21
... the tree is known by his fruit.—Matthew 12:33

Someone said that Jesus lost his temper when he cursed the
fig tree. Jesus was angry—yes, very angry—but he did not lose
his temper. To lose one's temper is to lose self-control; and
self-control, writes Paul, is one of the fruits of the Spirit. The
whole life of our Lord is marked by a majestic self-control.
Behold him before Pilate and Herod—spat upon, insulted, faced
with false witnesses, and yet, silent. But Jesus was angry many
times—purposely angry. He was angry when he drove the
money-changers out of the temple. He was angry when he fired
his repeated "woes" at the Pharisees. And the blazing anger
which withered the fig tree to its roots will be remembered to
the end of time. These incidents illustrate God's anger with
those who, like the fig tree with its large and fresh leaves, promise fruit and give none—those who profess much but offer nothing to justify the promise of their profession. The heart of Jesus
beats with the heart of the multitudes who curse a barren,
hypocritical, worthless religion.

*O Lord, may I not let you down, and may I not let others
down who look to me for help and inspiration. Keep me from
professing more than I practice. Make my life consistent and
fruitful in every grace and good work.*

CHANGE

Examine yourselves. . . .—2 Corinthians 13:5

But we all . . . are being changed into his likeness from one degree of glory to another. . . .—2 Corinthians 3:18 (RSV)

Everyone is at some time disgusted with himself. Suddenly our eyes are opened, and we see our faults as they really are. The sight is not pleasant—pettiness, cowardice, lovelessness, pride, hardness of heart, unbelief, a critical spirit, jealousy, and so on ad infinitum. At such times one is tempted to turn away from the disagreeable picture and say, "Well, I am no worse than other people; no one is perfect." This reaction is cowardly, senseless and profitless. How much better to turn to God in faith. There is no one, absolutely no one, who cannot be changed by God. The conditions are an honest confession of our helplessness to change ourselves, a keen desire to be changed, and the placing of ourselves in God's hands with complete abandonment and expectation. That is faith. "Lord, Thou canst make me clean," cried the leper, and *he was clean!*

O Lord, you have the power to change me. You can destroy my bad habits; you can break the chains that bind me; you can transform my disposition. Dear Lord, I believe; help my unbelief!

BOTH

... he that loveth not his brother whom he hath seen, how can he love God whom he hath not seen?—1 John 4:20

Beloved, if God so loved us, we ought also to love one another.—1 John 4:11

It was a sunny day in the Bois de Boulogne, Paris, and a little girl was gaily rolling her hoop. Suddenly she stopped. Her eyes had been arrested by the sight of a man, filthy and in rags, who sat on one of the benches with his head between his hands and great tears falling from his eyes to the ground. She could play no longer—she must do something. Quickly I ran to the man (for I was that little girl), placed my hand on his knee and bending to look up into his face, said, "Ne pleure pas; Dieu t'aime et moi je t'aime aussi." (Don't cry; God loves you and I love you too.") I was rewarded by a big smile. That was my first sermon.

It is not enough to preach, "God loves you," to a suffering humanity—people will not believe it. They will laugh you to scorn. We must be able to add, "I love you too." God's love is *proved* by our love. Nor is it enough to say by acts of kindness and charity, "I love you," for man needs more than material aid; that is why social work so often fails. Man "cannot live by bread alone"—he needs food for the soul as well as for the body. We must add, "God loves you," and help people to believe it. In Europe the upheaval resulting from two wars made Christianity become again, as in its beginning, a matter between God and man and between man and his fellow. Reduced to its ultimate expression, Christianity is "God loves you" (as revealed in the gift of Christ), and "I love you too."

O Lord, help me to love people as people and because you love them. May I never forget that every human being is equally dear to your heart, regardless of worthiness. May I give love, your love and mine, and keep on giving.

STORM

So persecute them with thy tempest, and make them afraid with thy storm. Fill their faces with shame; that they may seek thy name, O Lord.—Psalm 83:15–16

Prophesy unto the wind . . . Come from the four winds, O breath, and breathe upon these slain, that they may live.—Ezekiel 37:9

"God washed the world last night," wrote the poet William Stidger about a storm. We may not like storms, but they are greatly needed. Even as the wind and the rain break off dead branches, wash away destroying insects from leaves, soften the earth to make it fertile, so do spiritual storms uncover for us hidden sin, wash us with tears of repentance, clear away clouds which hide the face of God, and give us a rebirth. Every genuine revival is a spiritual storm. People often resist such seasons of spiritual refreshing because they do not like for their routine to be disturbed. But God pity our woods and fields without storms, and our souls without revivals. Storms are unpleasant while they last, but oh the delight of the newness of earth, sea and sky after a storm.

One early morning I took a walk in a woods in Germany. The night before, a storm had raged. Soon I became conscious of a delicious fragrance in the air, and looking down I caught a gleam of white, here, there, everywhere—lilies of the valley! They were carpeting the woods. A little further down the way, I came across a great oak that had been split asunder. How startling! The same storm that shattered the oak had only served to refresh and beautify the delicate lilies. Why? The oak resisted the storm, but the lilies yielded to it. Don't resist God's storms in your life; they are his ministers to you.

O wind of God, blow through my soul; O lightning of God, strike sin in my heart; O rain of God, wash me and make me clean.

CONTINUANCE

Pray without ceasing.—1 Thess. 5:17

Evening, and morning, and at noon, will I pray, and cry aloud: and he shall hear my voice.—Psalm 55:17

What did Paul mean when he wrote to the first Christians that they should pray "without ceasing"? He surely did not expect them to spend their lives in the religious exercise of prayer. They, like us, had to earn their living. The answer lies in the nature of prayer. Prayer is many things, but essentially it is the breathing of the soul. As in physical breathing we exhale and inhale, so in prayer we cast out of our souls that which poisons them—hatred, envy, greed, fear—and we receive the life-giving oxygen of God's spirit. We cannot pray while thinking greedy, envious or unkind thoughts. And even as we breathe automatically, so may we pray instinctively, continuously. Our whole life may be so infused with the love of God that at all times and in all places—office, marketplace, home—we will subconsciously keep in touch with God. This is what the monk Brother Lawrence called "practicing the presence of God." When we keep in touch with him in the subconscious, his spirit will more and more penetrate and control the conscious. This is the meaning of prayer without ceasing, and it brings joy, spiritual power and victory.

O Lord, how true is the hymn, "I need Thee, Oh, I need Thee, Every hour I need Thee." Just as I need my hands, my feet and eyes, so do I need you. May I always keep in touch with you. May my life be one continuous prayer.

106

DESIRE

. . . he shall give thee the desires of thine heart.—Psalm 37:4

With my soul have I desired thee in the night; yea, with my spirit within me will I seek thee early.—Isaiah 26:9

The great mystic, William Law, tells us that everything in the spiritual life is dependent upon desire. How true this is. Even prayer without desire is not real. Jesus said, "What things soever *ye desire* when ye pray, believe that ye receive them and ye shall have them." He also said that only those who *hunger* and *thirst* after righteousness shall be filled. On the outside of that great art museum the Palais de Chaillot in Paris, these words are inscribed:

> It depends on him that passes by
> Whether I am tomb or treasure,
> Whether I speak or am silent.
> This depends solely on you.
> Friend, do not enter my portals without desire.

"You will seek the Lord your God," Moses told the people, "and you will find him, if you search after him with all your heart and with all your soul" (Deut. 4:29, RSV).

O Lord, may I desire you beyond all else. May my soul be consumed with a passionate hunger and thirst after goodness. Then I know I shall be satisfied, for you have promised.

NEED

Blessed are the poor in spirit: for their's is the kingdom of heaven.
—Matthew 5:3

As the hart panteth after the water brooks, so panteth my soul after thee, O God.—Psalm 42:1

"Blessed are those who feel their spiritual need," thus Edgar Goodspeed translates the first Beatitude. The original word *blessed* may be translated, "happy"; hence, "Happy are those who feel their spiritual need." No matter how sick a man may be, if he still has feeling, he has life. Even so, to *feel* one's spiritual need indicates spiritual life and a chance for growth and fulfillment. Jesus had this in mind when he said, "Blessed are they which do hunger and thirst after righteousness [uprightness, goodness] for they shall be filled." Self-satisfaction and complacency mean a cessation of development; even worse, since in all life there is no standing still, they result in a going backward and a loss of any advance already made. Finally, they result in spiritual death. A difficult saying of Jesus may be applicable here: "For to him who has will more be given . . . but from him who has not, even what he has will be taken away" (Matt. 13:12, RSV). To be content with one's spiritual status is pride, man's most dangerous enemy, so this Beatitude might also read, "Happy are they who have no spiritual pride." It is fitting that the first of Jesus' "Blesseds" should have been given to the humble, for humbleness of spirit is the requisite for receiving every other blessing offered in the Beatitudes. Tom Thomas, a Welsh miner, who before his conversion was a crude and coarse sinner, became a living illustration of this truth. He learned to read that he might study the Scriptures. He was "humble-minded" (Phillips translation), radiantly happy, and certainly "owned" the kingdom of heaven.

O God, help me realize my spiritual need: save me from apathy, indifference and pride. The possibilities of my spiritual growth are infinite. Forbid that I should consider myself to have attained.

SORROW

... Jesus went unto them, walking on the sea.—Matthew 14:25

Weeping may endure for a night, but joy cometh in the morning.—Psalm 30:5

When in the depths of grief I wrote a poem, the first stanza of which reads:

> Sorrow is like a deep, deep sea,
> With waves that toss and moan:
> The sky above is dark with fear,
> And I am all alone.

The aloneness of sorrow is one of its most agonizing characteristics. Not even the dearest and nearest can enter into our pain. No one can subdue those tremendous waves of grief that rise within us and threaten utterly to overwhelm our spirit, mind and body. It was at such a time that I suddenly thought of the night when the disciples' frail bark was threatened with disaster by a storm, and when they saw someone coming to them walking on the water. Like those disciples I longed for the presence of Christ and stretched out my hands to him. He came, and the storm in my soul died down. He is the only one who can reach us through the storm of sorrow, the only one whose feet can step on those terrifying waves, the only one who can subdue our passionate grief and bring us peace—a peace not necessarily of understanding but born of confidence—confidence in his love for us. The last two stanzas of the poem read:

> If but my hand is held in Thine
> I will not ask to know
> The "Why" of wind and stormy wave—
> Dost Thou not will it so?

> All that I ask, most blessed Lord,
> But this must needs be mine,
> Is consciousness of Thy dear love
> Of my hand clasped in Thine.

SEED

... whosoever shall lose his life ... shall save it.—Mark 8:35

... underneath are the everlasting arms.—Deuteronomy 33:27

A grain of wheat, a single seed—how small and insignificant! It remains alone and is useless, said Jesus, unless it falls into the earth and dies (John 12:24). But if it dies, it bears much fruit, and a harvest ultimately results from one seed. The key words are *fall into the ground*. The seed does not fall into space; it falls into the rich full earth, and it is the union of the earth and the seed that makes the harvest. We human beings hate to let go. It is a blow to our pride to admit defeat. We insist on saving ourselves, and yet we cannot do so. Why not throw up our hands, surrender, fall, but not into nothingness—fall into God! He is the ground. In him we suddenly find rest; we are released from the prison of lonely self. Our weary struggle ends. He takes over, and in our union with him we find ourselves infinitely enriched. We come alive and begin to grow and to enrich others. Of itself the seed can do nothing—it needs the ground. But neither can the ground bring forth without the seed. They were made one for the other.

You may not realize it, but you need God and he needs you. There is no greater experience in human life than that of the marriage of the soul with God. Alcoholics Anonymous is one example that holds the secret of the deliverance of so many. They found that what could not be done by them alone they could accomplish with God. "If God be for us who can be against us?" exclaimed Paul, and also, "I can do all things through Christ who strengthens me."

Dear Lord, I feel small and helpless like the seed. It is true I can do nothing by myself to save myself. I am my own prisoner, my own slave, and my own taskmaster. But you are able to do exceeding abundantly above all I can ask or think by your power that works in me. And so I let go; I let you take over. I fall into the rich full soil of your love and grace.

111

SNAPPED

The fear of man bringeth a snare.—Proverbs 29:25

The Lord is my light and my salvation; whom shall I fear? the Lord is the strength of my life; of whom shall I be afraid?—Psalm 27:1

Sometimes small incidents have large effects. A woman weeping tears of joy told me her experience. She said, "While you were preaching on Pentecost, you leaned over the pulpit and snapped your fingers, saying, 'When the disciples were filled with the Spirit of God, they did not care *that* (snap!) what people said about them.' In that instant I was gloriously delivered from a bondage I had suffered for years: the fear of my neighbors and of what they might think or say about me. I feared one person in particular and suffered agonies because I had been told of her criticisms of me. You cannot imagine how happy I have been from the moment you snapped your fingers." Fear is a slave-driver and a most cruel master. There is only one whose opinion of us really matters. If we do that which is pleasing in his sight we need not fear what man may think or say about us. "Stand fast therefore in the liberty wherewith Christ hath made us free, and be not entangled again with the yoke of bondage" (Gal. 5:1), writes Paul to the Galatian Christians. Learn to snap your fingers playfully, joyfully, lovingly.

Dear Lord, deliver me from every bondage. Break every chain of fear, and release me from every hurt caused by self-love. May I seek only the praise which comes from you. This day I will go forth free as the birds that fly because you have set me free.

112

FELLOWSHIP

That they all may be one; as thou, Father, art in me, and I in thee, that they also may be one in us: that the world may believe. . . .—John 17:21

Behold, how good and how pleasant it is for brethren to dwell together in unity!—Psalm 133:1

A certain Episcopal church in the South has instituted a new means of ministering to the spiritual needs of the people: a group of the laity—men and women—calling themselves, "A Fellowship of Need." These people from all walks of life and from various churches share their spiritual experience with other lay men and lay women. They share what they *know* in their lives of God and of the saving and transforming power of Christ. This is a return to early Christianity, predating the organized church with its hierarchy and sacraments, predating the Reformation with its Bible-centered theology. Unfortunately the Church today does not speak with a united voice. There are over two hundred member-churches of the World Council of Churches, not counting those outside it. Christians do not have a general agreement about the Bible. They are divided on theological issues. But Christians, real Christians everywhere, are united in their faith in and experience of Christ and his saving grace. In this they are one; in this they have a positive and world-transforming message. And this message has been entrusted by our Lord to the laity, both men and women (Acts 1:8 and 2:17–18) whatever denomination. The united Christian witness of the laity is the only answer to the united and vocal secularism and atheism of the world.

Dear Lord, give me the humility to appreciate the value of fellowship with my fellow Christian no matter what his or her denomination or race, and help me to be ready at any time and in any situation to give my witness in my conduct as well as in my words—my witness as your disciple.

RELATIVES

For neither did his brethren believe in him.—John 7:5

What are these wounds in thine hands? Then he shall answer, Those with which I was wounded in the house of my friends.—Zechariah 13:6

Those we love most have the power to hurt us most. Family discords and quarrels are the hardest to bear. Many stalwart Christians, able to stand the assaults of adversity, of sickness, or of other disaster, have been utterly defeated by family trouble. Did Jesus know anything of this? We read that his brethren did not believe in him; they criticized him, called him mad and even wanted him arrested. How much of suffering and loneliness is hidden in the years he lived with his family as a carpenter? And he spent thirty years at home before starting his public ministry of only three short years! Shall we not learn from our Lord? First, he never fought back. Silence is a great weapon—not the silence of sulkiness or resentment, but the silence of self-control, of love and patience. Second, he never compromised. On one occasion he said, "For whosoever shall do the will of my Father . . . the same is my brother, and sister, and mother" (Matt. 12:50). At all cost we must do the will of God, quietly, perseveringly, in the spirit of love and the confidence of faith; we must go on doing that which we know is right, regardless of opposition or criticism. And we may be amazed to find that we have won the members of our own family. The very brethren that had called Jesus mad were in the Upper Room with his mother and the other disciples, and together with them received the Holy Spirit on the day of Pentecost.

Lord Jesus, those you loved hurt you. Help me to be strong, forgiving and loving, no matter how deeply I am hurt. You can cause me to rise above pain and disappointment, and experience the victory of love which "suffers long and is kind."

114

PEBBLE

So David prevailed over the Philistine . . . with a stone.—1 Samuel 17:50

For who hath despised the day of small things?—Zechariah 4:10

"And David chose five smooth stones out of the brook" (1 Sam. 17:40)—pebbles such as he had loved to play with as a child—small, smooth, shiny. How often he had practiced the swift twirling of the sling above his head, the sure and deadly aim at bear or lion! And now that the armies of the Lord were confronted with the mighty Goliath he was unafraid. He knew that one of those pebbles would be sufficient to slay the giant. If one failed to reach its target, another would surely do so.

Our Goliaths are many and they appear in different guises, but the pebbles in God's brook can slay them. The giant *fear* will go down before the tiny pebble of faith. The pebble of delight in the goodness of God will slay the giant *despair*. "Delight thyself also in the Lord; and he shall give thee the desires of thine heart" (Ps. 37:4). The pebble of joy, the "strength" of Nehemiah, brought low the giant *ridicule*. "The joy of the Lord is your strength," he exclaimed to his men (Neh. 8:10). Try the pebble of love against the giant *hate*. "Love never faileth" (1 Cor. 13). Practice doing good to the very ones you are tempted to hate and to those who despitefully use you. Saul's armor was only a hindrance to David—the arm of flesh will fail you. Try God's pebbles! They are mighty for the slaying of your spiritual enemies.

O God, fear of the Goliaths in my life has blinded me to the divine resources that lie at my hand. Open my eyes that I may see the small, but mighty, pebbles ready to be used in slaying my Goliaths.

FIGHT

I have fought a good fight. . . .—2 Timothy 4:7

I therefore so run, not as uncertainly; so fight I, not as one that beateth the air.—1 Corinthians 9:26

The Christian life is a spiritual warfare. "Our fight is not against any physical enemy," writes the Apostle Paul, "it is against organizations and powers that are spiritual . . . spiritual agents from the very headquarters of evil" (Eph. 6:12, Phillips). To be a Christian is a challenge to courage and to sacrifice. The early Christians knew this and so do millions of Christians in contemporary Europe. But the Church in America seems largely to have forgotten it. Here the Church stands in danger of being defeated by its very success and by the emphasis on the ease and comfort of its members. We do not have to suffer the loss of all things, torture, or even death for our faith, but we should remember that we are nevertheless challenged to fight. Our worst enemies are within us. Secret sins make cowards of us all. Some would rather meet a lion than come to grips with their own weaknesses and failures, but we are bidden to be "good soldiers of Jesus Christ." There is no thrill greater than that of laying our spiritual foes in the dust. Paul, the great warrior, wrote: ". . . we are more than conquerors through him that loved us" (Rom. 8:37), and he showed us the way to fight for a victory when he told us to be armed with "the whole armor of God" (Eph. 6:11), not your armor, not mine—not merely our own courage, strength or determination—but the armor of God. "Yea, by thee I can crush a troop; and by my God I can leap over a wall" (Ps. 18:29, RSV).

O Lord Christ, you who are the captain of my salvation, save me from self-pity, complacency and cowardice. Put strength in my spiritual muscle and toughness in my moral fiber. Clothe me with your armor of faith, truth, peace and salvation, and with the sword of the Spirit—your Word. May I daily make war on my enemies and yours, rejoicing in the assurance of victory.

SEX

Do not cheat each other of normal sexual intercourse. . . .—1 Corinthians 7:5 (Phillips)

Sex is a most beautiful gift from God, bringing ecstasy, comfort, joy and peace to both man and woman. God said, "They shall be one flesh." However, the blessings of sex depend on its manifestations being the expression of genuine love. When separated from the divine intention, love and marriage, sex becomes degrading, destructive, horrible. It may either exalt man or drag him down into the pit of hell. Like fire, in its proper place and controlled, sex serves man in a thousand ways. But out of place and uncontrolled, it destroys man and all he possesses. Even marriage does not prevent the misuse of sex. Only true love which is unselfish, devoted, tender and considerate makes sex what God intended it to be—the servant of human happiness.

A happy and normal sex life in marriage is the most beautiful and perfect human experience—beautiful in origin which is love, and beautiful in outcome which is children. These two make life complete. But to achieve a perfect marriage takes time, patience, determination, and, most of all, the grace of God.

Dear Lord, I thank you for the gift of sex. May I enjoy its blessings in a way that you can smile upon.

COURAGE

I can do all things through Christ which strengtheneth me.—Philippians 4:13

Be strong and of good courage; be not afraid, neither be thou dismayed: for the Lord thy God is with thee whithersoever thou goest.—Joshua 1:9

"There is no surrender in cell number 466." Those were the brave words uttered by Martin Niemoeller while a prisoner of Hitler in a concentration camp. This courage is of an entirely different nature from that expressed in William Ernest Henley's famous poem, "Invictus," in which he writes of a head "bloody, but unbowed," and which ends with the line, "I am the captain of my soul." The one courage is imparted by the Spirit of God; the other is self-created. The one has a divine foundation, which is rock; the other has a human foundation which eventually proves to be sand. The one lifts us above circumstances and gives us "songs in the night"; the other means a continuing conflict. The one means freedom from fear because it is *release from self;* the other means bondage to the domination of self and pride. Yes, Martin Niemoeller had the courage of declaring "no surrender" to man because there had taken place a complete surrender of his life to God, and this resulted in spiritual freedom, victory and peace.

O God, I dare not trust my own courage. Only as I keep my eyes fixed on you am I unconquerable, for you in me are greater than any who may be against me.

ONE

... this one thing I do ... I press toward the mark for the prize of the high calling of God in Christ Jesus.—Philippians 3:13, 14

Choose you this day whom ye will serve; ... but as for me and my house, we will serve the Lord.—Joshua 24:15

"This one thing I do," wrote Paul. "One thing have I desired of the Lord," wrote David. "You cannot serve two masters," said Jesus, and "If your eye be single your whole body shall be full of light." The word *single* in the King James Version is translated "sound" in the Revised Standard Version and "clear" in the Eastern text. How true it is that we cannot be sound in judgment or see our way of action clearly if we try to please many masters. We become confused and even sometimes sick in mind and body. This is natural since our spiritual state affects our mental and physical state. To be spiritually healthy, "whole," makes life a success regardless of material considerations. Jesus conditions even material success upon this singleness of heart. He said, "But seek ye first the kingdom of God, and his righteousness; and all these things [material necessities] shall be added unto you" (Matt. 6:33). God belongs in the center of life; everything else is part of the circumference. Put self in the center and God somewhere in the circumference and life becomes unbalanced, disordered and unhappy. Put God in the center and everything else will fall in its rightful place, and you will be a normal and happy Christian. Christians are men and women of one mind; rather, they are men and women of one person—Christ. "It is no longer I who live," exclaimed Paul triumphantly, "but Christ who lives in me; and the life I now live in the flesh I live by faith in the Son of God, who loved me and gave himself for me" (Gal. 2:20, RSV).

O my God, I am so often torn asunder by conflicting interests and demands. Create in me single-mindedness that I may always seek first your will and your glory. When confused may I keep you in my spiritual perspective; then I shall be flooded with light.

GROVE

Herein is my Father glorified, that ye bear much fruit. . . .—John 15:8

. . . every branch that does bear fruit he prunes, that it may bear more fruit.—John 15:2 (RSV)

Some things in life are obvious, and yet we do not really accept their truth. Behind my house in Florida is a grove of grapefruit trees, but it is pitiable, simply because the trees have not been pruned, sprayed or fertilized for years. There are parents who do not believe in discipline for their children—they say, "Let them be natural." And some professing Christians do not believe in holiness—"spiritual wholeness." They think it is enough to do "the best one can." Others resent the thought that God may permit suffering or that he may even will painful discipline for his children. Where then is the "pruning" which means pain? Where the "fertilizing" with the buried (surrendered) natural instincts? Where is the "spraying" with the tears of repentance and sorrow? No wonder some Christian lives resemble this pathetic grove—dead branches, strangling vines, wild undergrowth, and hardly any fruit. Did Jesus not say, "I am the true vine, and my Father is the vinedresser. . . . every branch that does bear fruit he prunes, that it may bear more fruit" (John 15:1–2, RSV)?

Dear Lord, may I not rebel against the pruning. You know the end from the beginning and what is best for me. If growth in grace must come through pain, I will accept the pain. I only ask one thing—let me bear fruit.

SHARING

Give to him that asketh thee, and from him that would borrow of thee turn not thou away.—Matthew 5:42

. . . if any one has the world's goods and sees his brother in need, yet closes his heart against him, how does God's love abide in him? Little children, let us not love in word or speech but in deed and in truth.—1 John 3:17, 18 (RSV)

No joy equals that of sharing—putting a room at the disposal of a homeless refugee, giving mother-love or father-love to some lonely child by adopting it, or even just giving a basket of groceries to a needy family that may be living around the corner. The look of love and gratitude in the eyes of those you are helping is a joy and a memory which brightens all of life. Everyone may prove the truth of the words of Jesus, "It is more blessed to give than to receive" [the word *blessed* also means "happy"]. We reap happiness wherever we sow it—wherever we give love, love comes back to us a hundredfold. And why not stretch out helping hands to those across the ocean whose needs and sufferings are almost beyond our imagination? Let us remember that Communism was originally a cry of anguish and rage against selfishness and greed. There would never have been an opportunity for Communism had professing Christians of means and in positions of power, in Russia and throughout the world, practiced the teachings of Jesus, had they adequately shared with the less privileged, and more important to the preservation of the dignity of man, had they provided means for the poor to help themselves. Today humanity is at the crossroads, and it behooves us who are Christians to be like our Lord in ministering to the needy. He said, "I came not to be ministered unto but to minister."

Dear Lord, make me quick to hear the cry for help, quick to notice need or want, and quick to do my part. May I know from experience the joy of sharing.

LAURA

... I know whom I have believed, and am persuaded that he is able to keep that which I have committed unto him. . . .—2 Timothy 1:12

... no one is able to snatch them out of the Father's hand.—John 10:29 (RSV)

It was late on a dark and stormy night in Newfoundland. The people had bundled up and gone home from the meeting. As I was leaving the church a woman slipped up in the darkness. "Is it too late for me to be saved," she whispered. "No," I said quickly, "it is never too late." "But I am Laura, the sinner of the town." "So am I a sinner," I answered, "so are we all apart from the grace of God." When I told my hostess who it was that I had invited to come to see me, she exclaimed indignantly, "She cannot come into my house." "I am sorry, but in that case, I will have to leave your house," I answered, "for I did not come to preach just to the church people of your town. You ought to be very glad that she wants to come." The unhappy woman came and was converted. In the following meeting she witnessed publicly to her experience. But the people did not believe her, nor would anyone give her a job although she had a child to support! She had a glorious voice but was refused a place in the church choir. I felt so ashamed for the "Christians" of the town. How I wish I had taken her and her child to my home in America! My heart ached when time came for me to leave. It was *she* who comforted me! "Never mind, honey," she said as the train was about to pull out, "I will sing in the heavenly choir; and as for the present, God will provide for me and my child. I will find honest work." I could hardly see her through my tears, but I could hear her voice above the noise of the departing train as she sang the little chorus she had learned in the meeting: "I'll keep my eyes on

God, I'll keep my eyes on God and my body shall be full of light."

Dear Lord, like Laura I will not let the opinions or criticisms or discouragings of other people rule my spirit. I will not look at myself, my past or my failings, for this is the way of defeat. Nor will I look at the future, for that is in your hands. I will keep my eyes steadfastly on you, knowing you are able to keep me from falling.

AWARENESS

Consider the lilies of the field, how they grow.—Matthew 6:28

And Isaac went out to meditate in the field at the eventide.—Genesis 24:63

Too readily do we let the big things of life blind us to the little things so necessary to our happiness. Large responsibilities, heavy cares, great sorrow, are allowed to blot out the glory of the evening star, make us deaf to the song of a mockingbird, blind to the opening of a rosebud in our garden, unmindful of a cup of tea thoughtfully offered. How different was our Lord who noticed the wild flowers, the little children and the birds. God has surrounded us with the gentle beauties of nature and with a thousand and one little blessings and pleasures that bring us healing and comfort and renew our youth. To neglect these free gifts is not only ungrateful, it is also injurious to our spiritual health and moral balance. A businessman may in reality be committing suicide by ignoring the innocent joys of life and nature while keeping his nose to the grindstone for the sake of money. A harassed mother becomes cantankerous and cross and loses her hold upon her children because she does not relax with them in the everyday joys of life. It pays to tear oneself away from encumbrances, if it be only for a moment, and to bathe one's soul in the beauty of nature, or to reestablish contact with the small and so often unappreciated blessings of life all around us.

Blessed Master, open my eyes that I may see the loveliness in little things about me. Touch my ears that I may hear the music in the wind and in the laughter of a child. May I never lose my awareness of those riches which you have so freely lavished upon me.

126

DYNAMIC

... be filled with the Spirit.—Ephesians 5:18

... that ye might be filled with all the fulness of God.—Ephesians 3:19

The consciousness of God within is the secret of a dynamic life for the Christian. Some may know God as Father and Christ as Savior but still be strangers to the Holy Spirit as God present in their lives. No mother is satisfied for her child merely to have "a little" life; it is the overflowing energy that counts, the "extra" which makes all the difference, especially when illness attacks. So it is with the Christian—the fullness of the Holy Spirit in him is the "life more abundant" that Jesus spoke about, and it acts as a buffer between him and sin. When filled with the Spirit the Christian will not be a disappointment to himself, to those around him or to God. In the Garden of Gethsemane the disciples failed Jesus, but after Pentecost they changed history. A superficial Christian experience is certainly inadequate to meet the challenges of our atomic age. We need to be vital, alert, adventurous and dynamic if we are to minister to the spiritual needs of modern man. Our generation is asking whether Christians can answer the deep questions of the soul and solve agonizing human problems. They can but only when they are filled with the Spirit of God.

Lord, give me the fullness of your Spirit that I may be a healer of wounds, a minister to the needs of my fellows, and a medium of your grace.

CEMETERY

. . . whosoever liveth and believeth in me shall never die.—John 11:26

And I heard a voice from heaven saying unto me, Write, Blessed are the dead which die in the Lord from henceforth: Yea, saith the Spirit, that they may rest from their labours. . . .—Revelation 14:13

Sitting in a beautiful cemetery filled with great old trees and gorgeous flowers, I was suddenly overwhelmed with the realization that a cemetery is not necessarily a place of sadness. It may be good for the soul. Meditating here, one may be reminded of the blessedness of rest when the storms, conflicts and turmoil of life are past; one may rejoice in the memory of some beloved life well lived, of a conquering spirit that never dies; one may contemplate the blessedness enjoyed in the presence of the Lord when we shall know as we are known; one may be comforted by the realization that "all things work together for good to them that love God." Most important, one may be solemnized by the thought of the pricelessness of time and spurred to "redeem the time" that life, whether long or short, may be most worthwhile.

O Lord, may I not fear death but know it for what it is—the opening of a door into a fuller and more glorious life.

SINGING

... his song shall be with me. . . .—Psalm 42:8

It is a good thing to give thanks unto the Lord, and to sing praises unto thy name, O most High.—Psalm 92:1

Have you tried singing a song when you are discouraged? You may say, "That is just the time I cannot sing." There is a little chorus I love to sing at such times: "Keep on praising God; When the black dogs bark In the midnight dark, Keep on praising God. Keep on praising God; When your feelings say That you cannot pray, Keep on praising God. When you feel the wrong that would quench your song; Till the battle's done and the victory won; . . ." Perseverance will bring victory; dark doubts and fears which paralyze and threaten defeat will vanish, and the sunshine of God's smile will warm your soul again. There is great power in song. David knew this. He wrote in his psalm, "In the night his song shall be with me." In the night we need a song. Are you troubled with sleeplessness? Try remembering a hymn and singing it in your heart. "Count your blessings, Name them one by one. And it will surprise you what the Lord hath done."

My Father, I thank you for song, for the joy of singing and of hearing others sing, for the healing virtue of music, for the lifting power of praise.

FISHING

... it is hard for thee to kick against the pricks.—Acts 9:5

... henceforth you will be catching men.—Luke 5:10 (RSV)

The greatest fun in fishing begins when the fish is on the hook—then it jerks, plunges from side to side and fights violently. Great skill is required on the part of the fisherman to land his fish. Are you on God's hook? Perhaps that is why you are criticizing the minister, the church, the evangelist, or even your best friend. Some actually become violent in their fury because of the secret accusations of conscience. At the beginning of a meeting in a Canadian city excited people came to me and said, "Doctor ——— is here." He was evidently a great doctor but also famous for his sins. He came regularly. Then one night people came to me distressed: "He is not here." "Don't worry," I answered, "he'll be back." I knew God's hook was in him. He came back, the fish was caught, and he became a power for good in that city. Thousands fight God—fight him in all sorts of ways—but I have noticed, as in the instance of Paul, that the hardest fighters, when they surrender, become the best disciples. God knows that too.

Lord, have I been fighting you? Have I been resisting unconsciously the prodding of your Spirit? If so, I give up, I surrender, and pray that you will have your way with me.

130

ACCORD

These all continued with one accord in prayer and supplication, with the women, and Mary the mother of Jesus, and with his brethren.—Acts 1:14

And when the day of Pentecost was fully come, they were all with one accord in one place.—Acts 2:1

One accord—these two words reveal the secret of the mighty spiritual conflagration which marked the birthday of the Church on the day of Pentecost. They were of *one accord:* Peter (a fisherman), Luke (a doctor), Matthew (a publican)—one hundred and fifty men of various backgrounds and dispositions; and the women too, Salome (rich), Martha (a housewife), Mary (the mother of Jesus), all welded into one —one in love, in faith and hope and purpose. It had taken many days of prayer, heart searching, perhaps mutual confession and tears and much spiritual adjustment to achieve this oneness, but the moment came when suddenly they were one—one with God and one with each other. In that moment the spiritual positive and negative poles met and the divine bolt fell from heaven setting them, and afterwards their world, on fire! That was the purpose for which Jesus prayed, "That they might be one, even as we are one that the world may believe that thou hast sent me." When the world sees this *oneness,* the world does believe.

Lord, help me to remove that which stands between me and my fellowman, especially my fellow Christian. No matter if he slams the door in my face, let me do my part to be reconciled to my brother and leave the rest to you.

BROKEN

... a broken and a contrite heart, O God, thou wilt not despise.—
Psalm 51:17

Thus saith the high and lofty One the inhabiteth eternity, whose
name is Holy; I dwell in the high and holy place, with him also
that is of a contrite and humble spirit. . . .—Isaiah 57:15

The spear of wheat grows out of the broken seed. It was only
the broken bread in the hands of Jesus that could feed the multitude. Job was broken by the hand of God until he gave up and
cried, "I abhor myself" (Job 42:6). And then we read, "The
Lord blessed the latter end of Job more than his beginning"
(Job 42:12). We need to be broken, and broken again and yet
again, for by nature we are hard and unbending, stubborn and
rebellious, a "stiff-necked" people and "do always resist the
Holy Spirit." Not only should we be broken, but it is necessary
for us to *remain* so, if the Lord is to make his dwelling with us
and use us. We get mended too quickly! The blessing is in the
breaking, for the breaking *itself* is a blessing. This is illustrated
in countless Christian lives. I would mention one: Dr. Reinold
von Thadden-Trieglaff, Doctor of Jurisprudence and founder
of the great *Kirchentag* (the bi-yearly meeting of hundreds of
thousands of lay Christians in Germany), was two years in a
Siberian war camp, three of his sons were killed in the war, he
lost all his possessions, a beloved sister was accused by the Nazis
of being a spy and beheaded, and finally his health gave way.
It was while in a hospital bed, broken in heart and in body, that
the vision of *Kirchentag* came to him. When we take the breaking from the hand of God, then it becomes a blessing to
us and brings blessings to others.

*Dear Lord, I need your help that I may not rebel against suf-
fering, testing or grief. May I trust you completely to turn evil
into good for my blessing and the blessing of others.*

JAWBONE

And he found a new jawbone of an ass. . . .—Judges 15:15

Whatsoever thy hand findeth to do, do it with thy might.—Ecclesiastes 9:10

Was there ever a more original song than Samson's when celebrating his victory over the Philistines? "With the jawbone of an ass," he exulted, "heaps upon heaps, with the jaw of an ass have I slain a thousand men" (Judg. 15:16). Alone and unarmed Samson faced an army coming up against him. He looked around. What weapon could he use to defend himself? Suddenly he spied a jawbone on the ground. Nothing could be more contemptible or seemingly useless, but in the hands of Samson, the giant of strength, it proved sufficient. The decisive factor was not the weapon but the hand of him who used it. Great spiritual battles have been fought and amazing victories won with poor weapons in the hands of those strong in faith and love. David Livingstone in Africa, Hudson Taylor in China, Adoniram Judson in Burma, Kagawa in Japan, and Niemoeller in Europe, had practically nothing as instruments, but in the power of the Spirit and Word of God they achieved wonders in human helpfulness and kept the light of the Gospel burning in the darkness. The spirit in a man transforms the means. This is true of everyone who seeks to do his bit for God and humanity, whether in manual, mental or spiritual labor. The cathedrals of Europe owe their inspiring grandeur to humble chisels and hammers in the hands of dedicated craftsmen. Service may be lowly, the means weak, but the realization that every part of life may be dedicated to God glorifies the means and makes us effective in defeating his and our enemies.

O God, may I never forget the dignity of my humanity and that all work done with a spirit of love for you and for my fellowmen, though the means may be humble, is acceptable to you.

133

MUSHROOM

. . . work out your own salvation with fear and trembling: For it is God which worketh in you both to will and to do. . . .—Philippians 2:12, 13

. . . God hath chosen the foolish things of the world to confound the wise; and God hath chosen the weak things of the world to confound the things which are mighty; and base things of the world, and things which are despised, hath God chosen, yea, and things which are not, to bring to nought things that are.—1 Corinthians 1:27, 28

The mushroom is a largely forgotten little plant. It grows in the darkness of woods or caves. Suddenly, silently, it appears and grows so rapidly that its name has become synonymous with speed. It flourishes, transforming manure and other "despised" and "waste" materials into a vegetable of remarkable nutrient and medicinal properties. The mushroom may be proved to provide the answer to the problem of many of man's as yet mysterious ills. Like the mushroom, though in a hidden and lowly place, someone may, in cooperation with God's creating and re-creating power, become a means of blessing and enrichment to his fellowman. The Savior of the world was born in a stable. Great men of history, such as Lincoln, have had the humblest of beginnings and have also been humble in spirit. Unexplored possibilities, intuitive genius, creative greatness, all hidden, may be brought to light and developed by the cultivating hand of God if (and it is a big IF) that person will, in humility, work cooperatively with God, even as the mushroom does with nature.

Lord, have your way with me—enlighten me, inspire me, guide me, use me. Make me to serve my generation in whatever way I can best do so.

FLYING

Thou fool, this night thy soul shall be required of thee.—Luke 12:20

For what is your life? It is even a vapour, that appeareth for a little time, and then vanisheth away.—James 4:14

After the first nervousness of taking off, flying gives me a great sense of peace. I feel completely helpless, therefore, in the hands of God. Is this not true of all life? Whether on the ground or in the air, whether in the home, office or car, how little we can control our span of life. Hence it is most important that we live in such a manner that we can "close the book" at any time and feel we have done a good job. The most worthwhile thing we can do with life is to do the will of God and so bring joy into the lives of others. This joy endures, whereas all else passes away. To love and serve and bless is our calling as Christians. Jesus said, "I am not come to be ministered unto but to minister." We are born for the same purpose. And there are countless ways in which we may minister—small ways and big ways. To love well is to live well; to live well is to love well. Let us love, and love, and love—even those who do not love us, thus shall we fulfill the royal law of God—the law which is the fulfilling of all law. Then our lives, whether they be short or long, will be well-rounded and complete.

Help me, O Lord, to live my life in the light of eternity, to do what I can to the best of my ability to serve you and my fellow-man, keeping in mind that I might at any time be called away. May I depend on your grace and strength.

PERFECTION

And above all these things put on charity [love], which is the bond of perfectness.—Colossians 3:14

Till we all come . . . unto a perfect man, unto the measure of the stature of the fulness of Christ.—Ephesians 4:13

There are those who dislike the term *Christian perfection* (otherwise called "holiness," or "sanctification"). Among objections given are that such an aspiration is presumptuous, that it is professed by some whose lives do not justify their claim, that the criterion is often held to be an outward, negative and superficial one—giving up dancing, cards, the theater, or other pleasures—that no one is perfect, that such spiritual excellence would make one unnatural or other than human. But underlying all objections, I believe, are impatience with ourselves because of our shortcomings and unwillingness to give up those things which we know to be wrong; for secretly do not most of us desire Christian perfection? If this is not so, why do we criticize others when they fail? Why do we struggle and strive to overcome our own failings? Why do we pray to be like Jesus? We are like the bad little girl who followed me from place to place until I asked her why she did so. She stopped short, struggled with her tears, crumpled her dress in her hand and then stammered, "I want to be good." True Christian perfection is not a cold, negative whiteness; it is the warm, red-blooded courageous goodness so perfectly defined in Paul's magnificent thirteenth chapter of First Corinthians. To practice love as it is therein described—that is Christian perfection.

Help me, O God, not to be overwhelmed by discouragement when I fail. I know that I can live a victorious life with the help of Jesus Christ, my Lord.

JOY

... that they might have my joy....—John 17:13

Thou hast put more joy in my heart than they have when their grain and wine abound.—Psalm 4:7 (RSV)

Jesus is thought of as a Man of Sorrows. It is too often forgotten that he also was a man of joy. His sorrows were not for himself; they were for others and for the world. As for himself he had no greater wish for his disciples than that they might have *his joy* in them that their joy might be perfect. In his last talk with them he spoke of joy five times (John, chapters 13, 14, 15 and 16), and in his last recorded prayer (John 17) he earnestly entreated his Father that they might possess his joy. Are not many of our troubles and sorrows caused by sin and self-love? These were not in Jesus. He could say, "I do always those things which please my Father." Even after the Last Supper, when facing the cross, he sang a hymn with his disciples. And the cross itself, the author of Hebrews tells us, was made bearable by a secret joy: "Who [Jesus] for the joy that was set before him endured the cross, despising the shame" (Heb. 12:2). The joylessness of many professing Christians has been a stumbling stone to unbelievers. And yet, joy is one of the insignia of the Christian faith. When listing the fruits of the Spirit in his letter to the Galatians, Paul gives to it the next place in importance to love. Since doing the will of his Father was the cause of the joy in Jesus, may we not find joy in the same way? When we run after joy it escapes us, but if we possess the root of joy—doing the will of God—we shall also have the fruit.

O my God, may I love your will with deep devotion. May I seek to know it and strive to do it so I may experience a joy that the world cannot give and cannot take away.

LILY

Consider the lilies of the field. . . .—Matthew 6:28

Wherefore, if God so clothe the grass of the field, which today is, and tomorrow is cast into the oven, shall he not much more clothe you, O ye of little faith?—Matthew 6:30

"Consider," said Jesus, "the lilies of the field." In obedience to him we will contemplate the lily of the valley. How does it grow? It does not "toil" nor "spin"; it does not strive or struggle to be a lily. It *is* a lily because it has the lily life. And even so, a Christian is a Christian because he has the Christ life. "Not of works," writes Paul, "lest any man should boast" (Eph. 2:9). A Christian is not made by self-effort, by the Church, by the Sacraments. He is *born* of the Spirit of God. He receives the life of God by faith. And how does the lily grow? It has thousands of little invisible hands with which it draws whiteness from the sun, vigor from the wind, freshness from the morning dew, food from mother earth. The lily is always drawing. The Christian also has an invisible hand—the hand of faith with which he may draw. You need courage; do not seek to work it up, but draw courage from the God of power. You need love and forgiveness —draw from the Christ who prayed, "Father forgive them for they know not what they do." You need patience, wisdom, grace—draw from God's abundant supply, for all things are yours when you are Christ's (1 Cor. 3:21, 23).

I thank you, O Lord, for the glorious lessons I may learn from your created Word—nature. May I have eyes to see and ears to hear your message in a snowflake, a blade of grass, a whispering brook, a lily.

138

LIFE

. . . that they might have life, and that they might have it more abundantly.—John 10:10

. . . it is no trifle for you, but it is your life. . . .—Deuteronomy 32:47 (RSV)

Life is our most precious gift from God. But many do not take time to "live"; they don't even take time to BE! They treat themselves as machines. They work till they are tired, then they wind themselves up to work some more. We are not machines, nor are we animals. We are made in the image of God with spirits through which we can know and touch God. But it requires determination not to allow ourselves to be robbed of the privilege to *be*, to *live*, to *think* and to *pray*. Granted that we don't have time, *we must make time!* It is a question of selection. We must put first things first. The Master asked what will it profit a man if he gain the whole world and lose his soul—what indeed? Take time—run away into the woods, gaze at the stars at night—listen to the voice of God in your soul and obey it. You will find that to assert the rights of your soul is infinitely worthwhile. When you come into your own spiritually, all life has a new meaning.

O God, my Creator, I thank you for the gift of life. May I value it aright—may I enjoy it, savor it and use it in a worthwhile way.

RESURRECTION

... it is I myself ... for a spirit hath not flesh and bones.—Luke 24:39

... he shewed himself alive ... by many infallible proofs. ....—Acts 1:3

One of the greatest evidences of the resurrection of Jesus is the change that this event caused in the disciple Peter. He had denied his Lord with curses and oaths, he had been plunged into the deepest despair, and had wept bitterly. But after the resurrection he wrote, "By his great mercy we have been born anew to a living hope through the resurrection of Jesus Christ from the dead, and to an inheritance which is imperishable, undefiled, and unfading" (1 Pet. 1:3-4, RSV). What a shout of triumph! The death of Jesus which had accentuated the night in Peter's soul is now followed by the stupendous victory of resurrection which floods him with light; and he too, as it were, is raised from the dead. From a coward cringing before the mocking laughter of a servant girl, he is changed to the bold apostle who on the day of Pentecost accuses a scoffing mob of the death of Jesus and preaches to them this same Jesus as the risen Lord. The change from despair to hope, from cowardice to holy boldness, from weakness to strength, from fear to faith, from spiritual death to life—all this the resurrection of Jesus accomplished for Peter and can accomplish for everyone. We are not worshipping a dead Lord but a living Savior.

O God, I thank you for the "living hope" that is mine through the resurrection of Jesus from the dead, and that "eternal life" begins now for me through faith in him. May those with whom I associate daily be conscious of this quality of life which is mine—a life more abundant and victorious, a life that soars and sings.

LAYMAN

... ye shall be witnesses unto me. ... —Acts 1:8

... ye are a chosen generation, a royal priesthood. ... —1 Peter 2:9

The late Archbishop William Temple wrote: "Neither prophetic nor evangelistic gifts are dependent upon the grace of orders [meaning ordination]." The effectiveness of lay witness and ministry has been proved again and again in the history of the Church. It was a layman, a merchant, Peter Waldo, who in 1170 sold all his goods and started an itinerant ministry, preaching the Gospel of Christ wherever he went. When the Pope forbade his doing so, Peter Waldo decided that he must obey God rather than man, broke loose from the authority of Rome, and proclaimed the Good News all over Italy. He and his followers, called Waldensians, were the first Protestant Christians in Europe. Throughout the centuries and in spite of unspeakable persecution, the Waldensians held high the torch of liberty and of a living faith based on the Word of God.

Many are the Christian movements that have been started by laymen. Just as important is the solid foundation in daily Christian living laid by laymen in commerce, industry, the professions, the factory, the shop and the home. Again quoting the Archbishop: "The laity can demonstrate the practical working of Christianity in the home, at their work and in all their social relationships." And, after all, is it not the actual daily working out of Christianity in the home, the office, the factory, that is the proof of its genuineness and power?

Dear Lord, may I remember that Jesus was a carpenter. You are no respecter of persons. Give me the courage, boldness, love and wisdom that I need that I may be used by you in my daily life to advance your kingdom. May I introduce you to my fellowmen and introduce them to you.

141

OIL

... ye have an unction from the Holy One.—1 John 2:20

... the oil of joy. . . .—Isaiah 61:3

When starting on our honeymoon, my newlywed husband was entreated by my young brothers to lend them his car. Being very susceptible at that time, he granted their request only to be advised, when we were far away, that my brothers had landed in the police courts! They were driving the car without oil and it stopped in the middle of the Chicago traffic! An engine, no matter how fine, must have oil if it is to run smoothly and not be ruined. Oil in the Scriptures is one of the symbols of the Holy Spirit. Many Christians are sadly lacking in this blessed oil. Their lives grind and creak with crossness and self-exasperating effort. Their useless struggles endanger their souls and the souls of others. A little compact car with oil will run better than a Cadillac without it. Try using the oil of God's Spirit—his love, his grace—in the work of your office, shop, or home. See what a difference it will make tomorrow morning if you start the day by being "filled with the Spirit"—the oil of joy, peace and power.

Dear Lord, sometimes life seems too much for me—the continuous effort, the grind of routine, the endless problems, the succession of crises, the weariness of the flesh and of the spirit! Pour into me the healing oil of your spirit that the complex machinery of my life may work smoothly and that I may be borne forward.

WIND

The wind bloweth where it listeth.—John 3:8

... who walketh upon the wings of the wind.—Psalm 104:3

In a New York City newspaper it was stated that the people crowding that great metropolis owe their health to the wind blowing in from the ocean which, like a broom, sweeps clean the air breathed by millions.

The wind! Have you ever seen or touched it? Do you understand it? And yet your very life depends on it. How great is its power! One day the wind walked down the Ohio River, lifted the roof neatly off my husband's stately family home, opened the trunks in the attic and scattered his aunt's yellowed, love letters, tied in pink and blue ribbons, all over the neighborhood causing her great embarrassment—that wind which one can neither see nor touch! Speaking of the wind Jesus said: "So is everyone that is born of the Spirit." On the day of Pentecost there was heard the sound "as of a mighty rushing wind" and the disciples, in the Upper Room, were filled with the Holy Spirit, the divine wind, *the breath of God* (Acts 2:2). Peter who had been a coward and denied his Lord because of the mocking of a servant girl, now preached with boldness, timid women prophesied, a multitude was converted, and the Church was born!

O God, let the wind of your spirit blow through the temple of my soul, blowing away the cobwebs of sin and self-love that cling there. I receive into myself your breath—your Holy Spirit—that I may live transformed by the power of your life.

WEIGHT

Let us lay aside every weight, and the sin which doth so easily beset us, and let us run with patience the race that is set before us.—Hebrews 12:1

The honest man comes to the light so that it may be clearly seen that God is in all he does.—John 3:21 (NEB)

Several scriptural passages seem to indicate that early Christians were sports fans. ". . . at the sports all the runners run the race, though only one wins the prize. Like them, run to win!" Christians were told. Athletes "do it to win a fading wreath; we, a wreath that never fades" (1 Cor. 9:24–25, NEB). Sports also inspired this familiar passage: ". . . seeing we also are compassed about with so great a cloud of witnesses" (KJV), "let us throw off every impediment and the entanglement of sin, and run with determination the race for which we are entered" (Heb. 12:1, Goodspeed).

Sitting among the "witnesses" the author of this passage had observed that the runners stripped themselves of all but a loincloth in order to be light on their feet. He used this example to illustrate to the disciples the necessity of laying aside every "weight," as they ran the Christian race.

Weights, as contrasted to sins, are whatever indulgences or habits we cling to which drag us down and make it harder for us to live a joyous, victorious Christian life. Though not sins, "weights" often lead to sin.

Anything that enslaves or entangles the Christian—cigarettes, cards, alcohol, fashion, any addiction, whatever it be—is a "weight" and impairs the successful running of the race. Furthermore, it disappoints the many "witnesses" who watch to

144

see how we run—of the past, the noble army of saints and martyrs and godly ancestors; of the present, those with whom we live or work; of the future, the yet unborn who will look to us for precedents and inspiration.

Blessed Master, my pet weight is ———. *Create in me a sincere desire to be rid of it. Give me the will to do your will and more love for my fellowman.*

GOODNESS

He hath shewed thee, O man, what is good; and what doth the Lord require of thee, but to do justly, and to love mercy, and to walk humbly with thy God.—Micah 6:8

Follow peace with all men, and holiness, without which no one shall see the Lord.—Hebrews 12:14

When Pope John XXIII died, the whole world wept. He was mourned by people of all walks of life, of all races, of all nations, and even more remarkable, of all religions. The reason for this universal grief was simply that the whole world recognized and honored his goodness. Methodist Bishop Fred Pierce Corson said of him that he made "goodness news." It was its complete naturalness and unassuming character that gave Pope John's goodness its greatest appeal. Hardened criminals wept when he spoke to them in jail. A little old woman hesitating in the crowd was invited by him to come close. He told Khrushchev's daughter that he prayed for the people of Russia. During the torture-filled hours of his last nights, he prayed for all the babies born that night, and his last breath bore the words uttered by his Master at the last supper: "that they might be one," a prayer for all Christians, not just Roman Catholics, for he called all Christians "brethren." Goodness is simply God in action. After all, is not goodness another name for *love*, the love of the thirteenth chapter of First Corinthians without which, from God's standpoint, knowledge, doctrine, gifts, even faith have no value? Goodness is greatness and beauty. It overshadows the greatness of power, knowledge and achievement, and its beauty surpasses that of music, art, even nature. It sounds like sweetest music; it resembles the most thrilling sunrise; its power can remove mountains. The world needs goodness more than anything else, it would solve its problems and heal its wounds. Tears can be shed for no better reason than for the passing of a good man or woman. However, tears are of little value unless they are also tears of longing for that same goodness to be manifest in our lives, for "without holiness no man shall see the Lord."

O God, that longing for goodness is mine and you have promised that those who hunger and thirst for righteousness (goodness) shall be filled.

GOVERNMENT

Blessed is the nation whose God is the Lord.—Psalm 33:12 (RSV)

Righteousness exalts a nation, but sin is a reproach to any people. Proverbs 14:24 (RSV)

Faith in God is the guarantee of freedom. This is indirectly stated in the Declaration of Independence, bedrock of the American Constitution. Paraphrasing: "Governments are instituted among men to secure to them those inalienable rights with which they have been endowed by their Creator." Suppose there were no Creator, no divine giver of human rights and liberties. On what ground would we defend those rights and by what authority would we prevent self-made "gods" or dictators from taking these from us? We would be deprived of a supreme and final court of appeals. And faith in God is the bedrock of morality, of law and respect for law. The atheist may well ask: "Who is Moses? He writes that adultery is sin. I am as good as he, and I say it isn't. Who is there to judge between us?" If God did not inspire the Ten Commandments, the question is logical. Belief in God gives dignity to man, raises him above the animal, inspires in him a respect for himself and his fellowman and for the moral law written on the tablets of his heart by the divine hand. "The law of his God is in his heart" (Ps. 37:31, RSV). Since faith in God creates respect for morality and for law and order can it not be said that faith in God is the spiritual foundation of good government? "When thy judgments are in the earth, the inhabitants of the world learn righteousness" (Isa. 26:9, RSV). And conversely when there is no fear of God and respect for divine law corruption prevails and governments fail. Historian Arnold Toynbee writes that "out of sixteen civilizations that perished, thirteen died of moral decay."

O God, establish your law in my heart. May I love it and live by it, and may our nation be mindful of its foundations laid in you.

148

LORD

The witnesses laid down their clothes at a young man's feet, whose name was Saul . . . and Saul was consenting to his [Stephen's] death. —Acts 7:58; 8:1

I am Jesus whom thou persecutest: it is hard for thee to kick against the pricks.—Acts 9:5

Saul rode furiously toward Damascus. His heart was red hot with rage against those Christians. Carrying special orders from the high priest, he could now have them torn out of their beds, out of their houses, beaten, bound, and dragged to Jerusalem. His fury had steadily mounted ever since he had stood guard and watched an angry mob stone young Stephen to death, and had heard him cry, "Lord, lay not this sin to their charge."

Suddenly a blazing light overpowered him. Blinded, he fell from his horse into the dust of the road. "Who are you?" he cried. "I am Jesus whom you persecute. It is hard for you to kick against the pricks." Instantly Saul's spiritual eyes were opened. This Jesus must be God, for only God could know what even he did not know about himself. It was true, his rage had been his kicking against the goad—a secret, gnawing suspicion that maybe by killing Christians he was fighting the very God whom he thought he was serving. "Lord," he cried trembling and astonished, "What will you have me to do?"

"LORD!" In the moment that Saul called Jesus "Lord" he became Paul. In that moment he was converted, which means "turned," as he was to turn thousands in the future, "from darkness to light, from the power of Satan to the power of God."

"What will you have me to do?" What a change! Into the dust fell Saul, the sworn enemy of the Christians. Out of the dust rose Paul, the "servant of all the saints." Into the dust fell the arrogant commander. Out of the dust rose the humble "bondslave" of the Lord Jesus. Into the dust fell one who did all things according to his own will. Out of the dust rose one who wrote, "I do all things through Christ who strengthens me." He now exemplified what he was to write to the Corinthian Christians: He that is in Christ is a new creation, old things are passed away, all things are made new (2 Cor. 5:17).

Lord Jesus, like Saul I would call you Lord, and henceforth have your will be done in my life and not my own.

UNKNOWN

... the goodman of the house.—Luke 22:11

And he took the cup and gave thanks.—Luke 22:17

No one knows his name or anything about him except that he put his room at the top of his house at the disposal of Jesus and his disciples. And though he might have disliked Peter and been suspicious of Judas, he did not discriminate. All who came with Jesus were welcome. Consequently, a surpassing honor is his. It was in his room that the sacrament of the Lord's Supper was instituted, and later, on the day of Pentecost, it was there that the Church was born. What a joy it must have been to him that his common things—his basin, his towel, his dish and cup—were used by the Master on the last night spent with his disciples! His things were forever after glorified. And they have played a most significant part in religious art and history. Even so when we put our ordinary possessions at the disposal of the Lord they are not ordinary any more; they become fraught with significance and are endowed with a feeling of eternity. Nothing is common when blest with his touch and used in his service.

It is with joy, dear Lord, that I put all I have at your service—my home, my business, my things great and small. I pray you will bless and use them for the happiness of others and for your glory.

151

OLD

You gave him length of days.—Psalm 21:4 (Living Bible)

Thus all the days of Enoch were three hundred and sixty-five years. Enoch walked with God.—Genesis 5:24 (RSV)

No one wants to get old. And yet everyone desires to live long and this naturally means old age. It is good to be reminded that each period of life—youth, the middle years and old age—may experience its own particular blessings.

Youth of the spirit—"Still bearing fruit in old age, still remaining fresh and green, to proclaim that Yahweh [God] is righteous" (Ps. 92:14, Jerusalem Bible). The secret of this spiritual youth is to remain in God's presence continually. David wrote, "Goodness and mercy shall follow me all the days of my life, [because] I will dwell in the house of the Lord forever" (Ps. 23:6).

Testimony of age—"Let me live to tell the rising generation about your strength and power, about your heavenly righteousness" (Ps. 71:18, Jerusalem Bible). "Prolong my old age, . . . and all day long my tongue shall be talking of your righteousness" (Ps. 71:21, 24, Jerusalem Bible).

Continuing joy—"My lips shall sing for joy as I play to you" (Ps. 71:23, Jerusalem Bible).

Humility and service—Jesus said: "I did not come to be served but to serve" (Matt. 20:28, Living Bible) and "He that is greatest among you shall be your servant" (Matt. 23:11). The service of the old is needed, and they can make life meaningful and a blessing for others until the end.

Precious Lord, may I rejoice in your goodness whether my life be long or short, and may I be given the privilege of service to my fellowman as long as I live.

152